BASIC GRAMMAR

A · N · D

USAGE

THIRD EDITION

PENELOPE CHOY

Los Angeles City College

JAMES McCORMICK

San Bernardino Valley College

Harcourt Brace Jovanovich College Publishers
Fort Worth   Philadelphia   San Diego
New York   Orlando   Austin   San Antonio
Toronto   Montreal   London   Sydney   Tokyo

ISBN: 0-15-504935-6

Library of Congress Catalog Card Number: 89-81002

Printed in the United States of America

Preface

The Third Edition of *Basic Grammar and Usage* retains the essential form of the earlier editions, but several improvements have been made. The first unit of the text, "Identifying Subjects and Verbs," which stresses the primacy of that skill, has been enlarged by a new lesson, "The Position of Verbals." The second unit on subject–verb agreement has been rearranged to bring like rules together. The final unit now includes an entirely new lesson on such matters as italics, colons, and quotation marks. All of the lessons have new expository material, new examples, and new exercises. This edition also adds ready-reference lists and charts of key material inside the front and back covers.

To make it possible for instructors to quickly reproduce Unit Tests, Diagnostic Tests, and Achievement Tests, the *Teacher's Manual* has been enlarged to an 8 1/2″ × 11″ format. And a brief introduction, with suggestions for using the text, has been added to the manual. Answers to "A" exercises are now included in the text.

This edition was planned by Penelope Choy and James McCormick. Penelope Choy aided in the revision of Unit One. James McCormick revised the remainder of the text and the *Teacher's Manual*.

The authors are grateful to the following instructors for reviewing the second edition and for suggesting many of the revisions in this edition: Carol O. Sweedler-Brown (San Diego State University), Dennis Gabriel (Cuyahoga Community College), David Pichaske (Southwestern State University), and Gwen Rowley (Mesa Community College). We also thank Thomas Chamberlain and Leonard Lardy, friendly critics at San Bernardino Valley College.

We are grateful to many individuals at Harcourt Brace Jovanovich: Bill McLane, senior editor and gray eminence of this edition; Karen Allanson, associate editor; Sheila Spahn, production editor; Sarah Randall, production manager, and Kay Faust, designer of our lovely new cover.

We also thank, of course, our spouses, Gene and Virginia, who have kept a sense of humor.

Penelope Choy
James McCormick

Preface to the First Edition

Basic Grammar and Usage was originally written for students in a special admissions program at the University of California, Los Angeles. As part of their participation in the program, the students were enrolled in a composition and grammar course designed to prepare them for the university's freshman English courses. When the program began in 1971, none of the grammar textbooks then on the market seemed suitable for the students, whose previous exposure to grammar had been cursory or, in some cases, nonexistent. As the director of the programs's English classes, I decided to write a book of my own that would cover the most important areas of grammar and usage in a way that would be easily understood by my students.

The original version of *Basic Grammar and Usage* received an enthusiastic response from the students and was used successfully throughout the three-year duration of the program. After the program ended in 1974, many of the instructors asked permission to reproduce the book for use in their new teaching positions. By the time copies of *Basic Grammar and Usage* reached Harcourt Brace Jovanovich in 1975, the text had already been used by more than 1,500 students in nearly a dozen schools.

Basic Grammar and Usage presents material in small segments so that students can master a particular topic one step at a time. The lessons within each unit are cumulative. For example, students doing the pronoun exercises for Lesson 19 will find that those exercises include a review of the constructions treated in Lessons 16 to 18. This approach reinforces the students' grasp of the material and helps them develop the skills they need for the writing of compositions. To make them more interesting to students, the exercises in four of the six units are presented as short narratives rather than as lists of unrelated sentences. Each lesson concludes with two exercises, which may be either used in class or assigned as homework. In addition, each unit ends with a composition that the students must proofread for errors and then correct to demonstrate mastery of the material.

Students who have never before studied grammar systematically will find that working through the text from beginning to end provides an insight into the basic patterns of English grammar. As one student commented on an end-of-course evaluation, "The most important thing I learned from *Basic Grammar and Usage* is that if you learn what an independent clause is, half of your grammar problems are over." On the other hand, students who do not need a total review of grammar can concentrate on the specific areas in which they have weaknesses. To help the instructor evaluate both types of student, the Instructor's Manual accompanying the text includes a diagnostic test and a post-test divided into sections corresponding to the units in the book. There are also separate achievement tests for each unit, as well as answer keys to the exercises presented in the text.

Although *Basic Grammar and Usage* is designed for students whose native language is English, it has been used successfully by students learning English as a second language. In addition to being a classroom text, *Basic Grammar and Usage* can be used in writing labs and for individual tutoring.

Many people have shared in the preparation of *Basic Gramamar and Usage*. I wish in particular to thank the instructors and administrators of UCLA's Academic Advancement Program, where this book originated. In revising the text for publication, I have been greatly helped by the suggestions of Regina Sackmary of Queensborough Community College of the City University of New York and by Elizabeth Gavin, formerly of California State University, Long Beach, who reviewed the manuscript for me. Sue Houchins of the Black Studies Center of the Claremont Colleges contributed many ideas and reference materials for the exercises. An author could not ask for more supportive people to work with than the staff of Harcourt Brace Jovanovich. I owe a special debt of gratitude to Raoul Savoie, who first brought the UCLA version of the text to the attention of his company. I also wish to thank Lauren Procton, who was responsible for the editing, and Eben W. Ludlow, who has provided guidance and encouragement throughout all the stages of this book's development.

Penelope Choy

Contents

*IDENTIFYING
SUBJECTS AND
VERBS*

1

Sentences with One Subject and One Verb

The most important grammatical skill you can learn is how to identify subjects and verbs. Just as solving arithmetic problems requires you to know the multiplication tables perfectly, solving grammatical problems requires you to identify subjects and verbs with perfect accuracy. This is not as difficult as it sounds. With practice, recognizing subjects and verbs will become as automatic as knowing that $2 \times 2 = 4$.

Although in conversation people often speak in short word groups that may not be complete sentences, in written English people usually use complete sentences.

A complete sentence contains at least one subject and one verb.

A sentence can be thought of as a statement describing an *actor* performing a particular *action*. For example, in the sentence "The man fell," the *actor* or person performing the action is the *man*. What *action* did the man perform? He *fell*. This *actor—action* pattern can be found in most sentences. Can you identify the actor and the action in each of the sentences below?

The artist painted.
The audience applauded.

The *actor* in a sentence is called the **subject.** The *action* word in a sentence is called the **verb.** Together, the subject and verb form the core of the sentence. Notice that even if extra words are added to the two sentences above, the subject–verb core in each sentence remains the same.

The artist painted portraits of famous people.
At the end of the concert, the audience applauded loudly.

You can see that in order to identify subjects and verbs, you must be able to separate these core words from the rest of the words in the sentence.

Here are some suggestions to help you identify verbs.

1. The *action* words in sentences are verbs. For example:

The team *lost* the game.
I *play* tennis every weekend.
This bank *offers* high interest rates.

Underline the verb in each of the following sentences.

This restaurant serves low-sodium meals.

Dieters count calories.

The employees want higher salaries.

2. All forms of the verb *be* are verbs: *am, is, are, was, were,* and *been.* For example:

Sam *is* happy.
The patient *was* very weak.

Verbs also include words that can be used as substitutes for forms of *be,* such as *seem, feel, become,* and *appear.* These verbs are called **linking verbs**.

Sam *seems* happy
The patient *feels* very weak.

Underline the verb in each of the following sentences.

I am nervous about my new job.

Paula becomes nervous during job interviews.

The witness appeared nervous during the trial.

3. Verbs are the only words that change their spelling to show tense. **Tense** is the time – present, past, or future – at which the verb's action occurs. For example, the sentence "We *work* for United Airlines" has a present-tense verb. The sentence "We *worked* for United Airlines" has a past-tense verb. Underline the verb in each of the following sentences.

I enjoy good books.

My children enjoyed their trip to Disneyland.

Our class meets three days a week.

My sister met me at the airport.

The school needs more teachers.

The car needed a new battery.

Identifying verbs will be easier for you if you remember that the following kinds of words are *not* verbs.

4. An **infinitive** – the combination of the word *to* plus a verb, such as *to walk* or *to study* – is *not* considered part of the verb in a sentence. Read the following sentences.

The police tried to capture the robbers.
The airline wants to raise its fares.

The main verbs in these two sentences are *tried* and *wants*. The infinitives *to capture* and *to raise* are *not* included. Underline the main verb in each of the following sentences.

Stella hopes to become a movie star.

Congress voted to change the federal income tax system.

5. **Adverbs** – words that describe a verb – are *not* part of the verb. Many commonly used adverbs end in *-ly*. The adverbs in the following sentences are italicized. Underline the verb in each sentence.

The doctor examined the patient *carefully*.

The instructor *patiently* explained the lesson.

The dog barked *loudly*.

The words *not, never,* and *very* are also adverbs. Like other adverbs, these words are *not* part of the verb. Underline the verb in each of the following sentences. Do *not* include adverbs.

My husband never forgets our anniversary.

The traffic moved very slowly.

I exercise regularly.

Dinner is not ready yet.

The students quickly finished the exercises.

Now that you can identify verbs, here are some suggestions to help you to identify subjects.

1. The subject of a sentence is most frequently a noun. A **noun** is the name of a person, place, or thing, such as *Laura, Dallas,* or *pencils*. A noun may also be the name of an abstract idea, such as *happiness* or *success*. Underline the subject in each of the following sentences *once* and the verb *twice*. Remember that the verb is the *action,* and the subject is the *actor*.

Martha supports two children by herself.

The car hit a telephone pole.

California produces most of the nation's artichokes.

Alcoholism ruined his career.

2. The subject of a sentence may also be a **subject pronoun**. A **pronoun** is a word used in place of a noun, such as *she* (= *Laura*), *it* (= *Dallas*), or *they* (= *pencils*). The following words are subject pronouns:

    I, you, he, she, it, we, they

Underline the subject in each of the following sentences *once* and the verb *twice*.

    He started a new job yesterday.

    It always rains during April.

    Last month I moved to a new apartment.

    They often argue about money.

    She is my best friend.

3. In **commands**, such as "Shut the door!", the subject is understood to be the subject pronoun *you*, even though the word *you* is almost never included in the command. *You* is understood to be the subject of the following sentences.

    Dial 911 in case of emergencies.
    Please lower your voice.

Underline the subject in each of the following sentences *once* and the verb *twice*. If the sentence is a command, write the subject *you* in parentheses at the beginning of the sentence.

    An earthquake shook the city.

    Help me!

    He jogs five miles every morning.

    Clean the stove after dinner.

Identifying subjects will be easier for you if you remember that the following kinds of words are *not* subjects.

4. **Adjectives** – words that describe a noun – are *not* part of the subject. For example, in the sentence "The young actress won an Oscar," the subject is "actress," *not* "young actress." In the sentence "A private college charges tuition," the subject is "college," *not* "private college." Underline the subject in each of the following sentences *once* and the verb *twice*.

Tuna casseroles often appear at potluck dinners.

Microwave ovens shorten cooking time.

Hot fudge sundaes are my favorite dessert.

The new fall fashions include both long and short skirts.

5. Words that show **possession**, or ownership, are *not* part of the subject. Words that show possession include nouns ending in an apostrophe (') combined with *s*, such as *David's* or *car's*. They also include **possessive pronouns**, words that replace nouns showing ownership, such as *his* (= *David's*) or *its* (= *car's*). Possessive pronouns include the following words:

my, your, his, hers, its, our, their

Since words that show possession are *not* part of the subject, in the sentence "My daughter wears glasses," the subject is "daughter," *not* "my daughter." In the sentence "Judy's landlord raised the rent," the subject is "landlord," *not* "Judy's landlord." Underline the subject in each of the following sentences *once* and the verb *twice*.

Stuart's snores annoyed his roommate.

Our team scored two touchdowns in the fourth quarter.

Egypt's pyramids attract many tourists.

His friends gave him a surprise birthday party.

Here is a final suggestion to help you to identify subjects and verbs accurately.

Try to identify the verb in a sentence before you try to identify the subject.

A sentence may have many nouns, any of which could be the subject, but it will usually have only one or two verbs. For example:

> The theater in my neighborhood offers a special discount to students and senior citizens.

There are five nouns in the above sentence (*theater, neighborhood, discount, students, citizens*), any of which might be the subject. However, there is only one verb—*offers*. Once you have identified the verb as *offers*, all you have to ask yourself is, "Who or what offers?" The answer is *theater*, which is the subject of the sentence.

Identify the subject and verb in the following sentence, remembering to look for the verb first.

> These luxurious apartments appeal to people with high incomes and no children.

Remember these basic points:

1. The action being performed in a sentence is the **verb.**
2. The person or thing performing the action is the **subject.**
3. A sentence consists of an *actor* performing an *action*, or, in other words, a **subject** plus a **verb.**

Since every sentence you write will have a subject and a verb, you must be able to identify subjects and verbs in order to write correctly. Therefore, as you do the exercises in this unit, apply the rules you have learned in each lesson, and *think* about what you are doing. Do not make random guesses. Grammar is based on logic, not on luck.

Underline the subject in each of the following sentences *once* and the verb *twice*. Add the subject *you* in parentheses if the sentence is a command.

That car costs too much for my budget.

Her pink and purple hair attracted a lot of attention.

Raw seafood sometimes contains harmful bacteria.

The dog's constant barking disturbed the neighbors.

Keep an eye on the traffic.

Sturdy, reliable appliances no longer seem to exist.

Love is blind.

EXERCISE 1A

Underline each subject *once* and each verb *twice*. Each sentence has only one subject and only one verb. *Remember to look for the verb first* before you try to identify the subject.

1. English is a very old language.

2. It resembles a tree with many roots.

3. The main root is Germanic.

4. Ancient Germanic tribes crossed the channel west of France.

5. These tribes were the Saxons, the Jutes, and the Angles.

6. They conquered the western island.

7. Their new land became "Angle-lond" or "Eng-land."

8. Their language gradually evolved into "English."

9. Other invaders came after the Anglo-Saxons.

10. Each invasion changed the language.

11. The Roman invaders added many Latin words to English.

12. Take Latin words like *circus* and *data*, for example.

13. Later French conquerors brought their language to England.

14. Modern English includes many French words like *menu* and *garage*.

15. English seems to accept foreign words easily.

16. Many other languages lent their words to English.

17. Arabic gave English the word *algebra*.

18. We borrowed *patio* and *rodeo* from Spanish.

19. Today's English vocabulary is a mixture of many languages.

20. Chinese is the language of the world's most populous nation.

21. But more people speak English as a second language.

22. This language opens many doors throughout the world.

23. Learn to use it well.

EXERCISE 1B

Underline the subject of each sentence *once* and the verb *twice*. Each sentence has one subject and one verb. *Remember to look for the verb first* before you try to locate the subject.

1. John Silva went to his first college class, Physics 100.

2. The physics teacher spoke to the class.

3. "Physics studies the basic structure of the universe.

4. This course is probably the most important in the catalog."

5. John's next class was History 100 with Dr. Gomez.

6. Dr. Gomez began his first lecture with these words.

7. "History studies the past to explain the present and future.

8. History's lessons are the most important and basic of all."

9. At 11:00 John entered his Psychology 100 classroom.

10. Dr. Harris started with several introductory remarks.

11. "Psychology gives us an indispensable understanding of human behavior.

12. This course is probably the most important course in college."

13. John ate some lunch before his last class, English 100.

14. He sat near the front in English.

15. The English professor's name was Dr. Hogan.

16. He called the roll.

17. Then Dr. Hogan opened his mouth to begin his lecture.

18. Suddenly he stopped.

19. "You just wrote something in your notebook, Mr. Silva.

20. Share your mindreading with the class, please."

21. John looked around at the class.

22. Then he read the words in his notebook.

23. "English is the most basic and important class in college."

EXERCISE 1C

Each group of words below can be made into a complete sentence by the addition of *one* word. The missing word may be a subject (a noun or a subject pronoun) or it may be a verb. Make each group of words a sentence by adding either a *one-word subject* or a *one-word verb*.

1. Jack _____ his homework quickly.

2. The _____ started at noon.

3. Last month they _____ to Boston.

4. Her _____ was a professional ball player.

5. My _____ was too salty.

6. A complete sentence _____ a subject and a verb.

7. His brother's _____ looked beautiful.

8. _____ is her uncle.

9. The Tiger's soccer team _____ its last game.

10. _____ that chair!

11. The boss angrily _____ a speech about productivity.

12. The boat's _____ fell in the water.

13. _____ was our babysitter.

14. Please _____ the potatoes.

15. The old gray car _____ in the street.

16. _____ is my hobby.

17. My _____ likes to watch old movies on TV.

18. Old soldiers never _____ .

19. Birds of a feather _____ together.

20. All _____ are created equal.

2

Multiple Subjects and Verbs

Some sentences have more than one subject. Others have more than one verb. Many sentences have more than one subject *and* more than one verb. The subjects in the following sentences have been labled with an ''S'' and the verbs with a ''V.''

```
S     V         V
I washed and waxed my car.
```

```
      S       S    V
My brother and his wife adopted a baby girl.
```

```
        S     V              S     V
The President gave a speech, and then reporters asked him questions.
```

```
        S      V         S        V
Tim's checks often bounce because he never balances his checkbook.
```

You can identify the pattern of a sentence by indicating how many subjects and verbs it has. Although in theory a sentence can have any number of subjects and verbs, the most common patterns are:

S-V	one subject and one verb
S-V-V	one subject and two verbs
S-S-V	two subjects and one verb
S-V/S-V	two subjects and two verbs

Underline the subjects of the following sentences *once* and the verbs *twice*.

The bright light bothered my eyes.

The bank opens at ten and closes at four.

Grenada and Mongolia use Walt Disney cartoons on their postage stamps.

The election was important, but few people bothered to vote.

Any group of words that contains *at least one subject and one verb* is called a **clause.** A single sentence may have one clause, or more than one clause:

S-V	one clause	The teacher spoke to the class.
S-V-V	one clause	Tom listened and laughed.
S-S-V	one clause	Carlos and Lisa arrived.
S-V/S-V	two clauses	Pete left / when the bell rang.
S-V-V/S-V	two clauses	Ron waited and listened, / but we left.

Later in the book we will study the different types of clauses to understand how they determine punctuation. But for now the important thing is to learn to find *all* the subjects and verbs in each sentence.

Something to keep in mind when looking for multiple subjects and verbs is that the *length* of the sentence won't tell you whether the sentence has one clause, or several clauses. Look at these two sentences:

We leave if it rains. (How many clauses?)
The tired old football coach slowly climbed up the long ramp. (How many clauses?)

The first sentence is short, only five words, but it has two S-V patterns and, therefore, two clauses (*we leave* and *it rains*). The second sentence is more than twice as long, but it has only one clause (*coach . . . climbed*). So don't be fooled by the length of the sentence: some short sentences have multiple subjects and verbs, and some long sentences have only a single clause (S-V).

The sentences below are skeleton sentences. That is, they are stripped down to only subjects and verbs and connecting words. Go through them underlining the subjects *once* and the verbs *twice*.

Luanne waited and waited.

Albert and Earnestina met and kissed.

The boy and the girl and the woman talked.

When it rains, it pours.

It pours when it rains.

We left after it rained.

Juan and we left after the rain started.

Della and Marie and Connie cried because George died.

Because George died, Della and Connie and Marie cried.

If you go, I stay.

Wendell awoke and yawned and stretched.

Wendell yawned and stretched after he awoke.

After he awoke, Wendell stretched and yawned.

Rise and shine! (Did you remember to put *You* in front?)

The practice sentences below have multiple subjects and verbs, but they also include the other types of words you studied in Chapter One. Before you try them, review that chapter quickly to remind yourself about **adverbs** and **infinitives**, which are never part of the verb, and about **adjectives** and **possessives**, which are not part of the subject. Underline verbs *twice*, subjects *once*:

Bill and Irene like to dance slowly.

The old man and the old woman were very good dancers.

Tanya and the tall stranger danced and talked to each other.

Gary waited, but his old flame never arrived.

If the textbooks arrive, go and buy one.

Go and buy your Spanish textbook if it comes today.

Jill's book fell, and the tall boy retrieved it.

The very forgetful history professor forgot to remember his wedding anniversary.

The history professor's wife remembered but said nothing.

The professor's wife remembered, but she said nothing.

His wife remembered and reminded him, and they went out to eat.

This very long sentence's verb is not really an extremely large word.

EXERCISE 2A

Underline the subjects of the following sentences *once* and the verbs *twice*. Remember not to include infinitives as part of the verb. To help you, the pattern of each sentence is indicated in parentheses.

1. Everyone's body needs exercise. (S-V)

2. Many "exercises" do little good for the body. (S-V)

3. Weightlifting makes large muscles, but large muscles are not necessarily a sign of good health. (S-V/S-V)

4. A healthy person has healthy vital organs, and so good exercise begins with the heart and lungs. (S-V/S-V)

5. Our lungs and heart take in and distribute oxygen for the whole body. (S-S-V-V)

6. Every single cell needs a continuous supply of oxygen. (S-V)

7. A good exercise works the heart and lungs energetically. (S-V)

8. This hard work increases the efficiency of our oxygen intake. (S-V)

9. As this efficiency increases, even more oxygen becomes available to our millions of cells. (S-V/S-V)

10. *Aerobic* exercise is a system of physical conditioning to guarantee a good supply of oxygen. (S-V)

11. Walking, running, dancing, swimming, or cycling are *aerobic* if they really work the heart and lungs. (S-S-S-S-S-V/S-V)

12. Each aerobic exercise expends a certain amount of energy. (S-V)

13. Special charts show these amounts for each activity. (S-V)

14. If you are a walker, you walk at a certain speed to get an "aerobic" effect. (S-V/S-V)

15. If you are a swimmer, you swim so many laps in a certain time to get the aerobic benefit. (S-V/S-V)

16. Aerobic exercise programs appeal to many people because the programs bring the joy of health. (S-V/S-V)

EXERCISE 2B

Underline the subjects of the following sentences *once* and the verbs *twice*. Some sentences have more than one subject, more than one verb, or both.

1. The Domingo Lopez family lived in Roswell, New Mexico.

2. Domingo owned an auto-body repair shop.

3. He loved to play golf and was a very good golfer.

4. The Lopezes had a baby girl, and they named her Nancy.

5. When Nancy was very small, her mother and father took Nancy with them to the public golf course.

6. She watched her parents and wanted to hit the ball too.

7. Domingo took some old clubs and shortened them for Nancy.

8. She loved to go to the course and play golf with her father.

9. He taught her to think about her shots and to plan them carefully.

10. Nancy became good enough to enter pre-teen golf tournaments.

11. When she was nine, she won the state pre-teen championship.

12. While she was in junior high, she began to play against women.

13. Nancy played for her high school boy's team and led them to the New Mexico State Championship.

14. Her mother and father wanted her to have a chance to play in national matches, so they used their savings to pay Nancy's expenses.

15. She justified their confidence and came in second in her first three national tournaments.

16. Soon she won her first big match in Florida.

17. In 1978 and 1979 Nancy entered fifty professional tournaments, and she won seventeen of them!

18. Nancy's first two years as a pro were the most spectacular start in the history of women's golf.

19. Today she reigns as one of the great golfers of history.

EXERCISE 2C

The following sentences need more than one subject, more than one verb, or both. Put *one* noun, *one* subject pronoun, or *one* verb in each blank to complete each sentence.

1. Last month Lanny _____, _____, and

   _____.

2. The _____ and the _____ jumped over

   the fence.

3. After Mark _____ his homework, he

   _____ his friend.

4. Lucy _____ Charlie and then _____

   him.

5. In 1986 the team _____ every game, but in 1987 it

   _____ every game.

6. _____, _____, and

   _____ always go to the mall together.

7. The singer _____ well, but the band

   _____ too loud.

8. The tall _____ and the short _____

   smiled.

9. _____ the dishes and _____ them.

10. In July we _____ to the beach and _____

in the waves.

11. Pat's _____ and Mike's _____ ran

away.

12. When the _____ started, we _____.

13. The very expensive new stereo _____ and

_____.

14. _____ the car and _____ me out!

15. My boss _____ a raise after I _____ the

most merchandise.

3

Distinguishing Between Objects of Prepositions and Subjects

One of the most common causes of errors in identifying the subject of a sentence is confusing it with a noun used as the object of a preposition. To avoid making this type of mistake, you first must learn to recognize prepositions and prepositional phrases.

Prepositions are the short words in our language that show the *position* or relationship between one word and another. For example, if you were trying to describe where a particular book was located, you might say:

The book is *on* the desk.
The book is *in* the drawer.
The book is *by* the table.
The book is *under* the notebook.
The book is *behind* him.

The italicized words are all prepositions. They show the position of the book in relation to the desk, the drawer, the table, the notebook, and him.

Here is a list of the most common prepositions. You do not have to memorize these words, but you must be able to recognize them as prepositions when you see them.

about	between	of
above	beyond	on
across	by	onto
after	concerning	out
against	down	over
along	during	through
amid	except	to
among	for	toward
around	from	under
at	in	up
before	inside	upon
behind	into	with
below	like	within
beneath	near	without
beside		

As you can see from the sentences describing the location of the book, prepositions are not used by themselves; they are always placed in front of a noun or pronoun. The noun or pronoun following the preposition is called the **object of the preposition.** The group of words containing the preposition and its object is called a **prepositional phrase.** Any words, such as adjectives or the words *a, an,* or *the,* which come between the preposition and its object are also part of the prepositional phrase. Read the following sentences, in which the prepositional phrases are italicized. Notice that each prepositional phrase begins with a preposition and ends with a noun or pronoun.

Julie studies *in the library.*
The children sat *beside their mother.*
Mike shares an apartment *with them.*
I drank two cups *of coffee.*

Some prepositional phrases may have more than one object.

The bank closes *on weekends and holidays.*
I like pizza *with pepperoni and anchovies.*

It is also possible to have two or more prepositional phrases in a row.

She sits *in the row behind me.*
The plane came *to a stop at the end of the runway.*

Circle the prepositional phrases in the following sentences. Some sentences may have more than one prepositional phrase.

We often walk along the beach.

The invitation to your party arrived in today's mail.

I drove around the parking lot for ten minutes.

The school closes during the months of July and August.

Construct sentences of your own containing prepositional phrases. Use the prepositions listed below. Make certain that each of your sentences contains at least one subject and one verb.

with: _____

_____

through: _____

_____

by: _____

_____

of: _____

_____

at: _____

_____

The words *before* and *after* may be used either as prepositions or as conjunctions (page 110). If the word is being used as a preposition, it will be followed by a noun or pronoun object. If the word is being used as a conjunction, it will be followed by both a subject and a verb.

As a Preposition	*As a Conjunction*

	S V
The movie ended *before midnight*.	*Before* he does his homework, he eats a little snack.

	S V
He retired *after his seventieth birthday*.	We left the restaurant *after* we finished dinner.

What do prepositional phrases have to do with identifying subjects and verbs? The answer is simple.

Any word that is part of a prepositional phrase cannot be the subject or the verb of a sentence.

This rule works for two reasons:

1. Any noun or pronoun in a prepositional phrase must be the object of the preposition, and the object of a preposition cannot also be a subject.

2. Prepositional phrases never contain verbs.

To see how this rule can help you to identify subjects and verbs, read the following twenty-four-word sentence:

> During my flight to Hawaii, the passenger in the seat beside me knocked a glass of orange juice from his tray onto my lap.

If you want to find the subject and verb of this sentence, you know that they will not be part of any of the sentence's prepositional phrases. So, cross out all the prepositional phrases in the sentence.

> ~~During my flight to Hawaii~~, the passenger ~~in the seat beside me~~ knocked a glass ~~of orange juice~~ ~~from his tray~~ ~~onto my~~ lap.

You now have only five words left out of the original twenty-four, and you know that the subject and verb must be within these five words. What are the subject and verb?

Read the following sentence, and cross out all of its prepositional phrases.

> At night the lights from the oil refinery glow in the dark.

If you crossed out all the prepositional phrases, you should be left with only three words — *the lights glow.* Which word is the subject, and which is the verb?

Identify the subject and verb in the following sentence. Cross out the prepositional phrases first.

During the summer a group of students from local high schools came to

the university for special classes.

If you have identified all of the prepositional phrases, you should be left with only three words — *a group* and *came.* Which word is the subject, and which is the verb?

Now you can see another reason why it is important to be able to identify prepositional phrases. It might *seem* logical for the subject of the sentence to be *students.* However, since *of students* is a prepositional phrase, *students* cannot be the subject. Instead, the subject is *group.*

Underline the subjects of the following sentences *once* and the verbs *twice.* Remember to cross out the prepositional phrases first.

The celebration of the centennial of the Statue of Liberty occurred in 1986.

A family with five children lives next door to me.

All of the students finished the exam within an hour.

Two spaces in the parking lot are for people with physical disabilities.

The museum's collection of paintings includes works by famous Spanish

artists like Goya and El Greco.

At the beginning of the winter, the lack of snow hurt business at ski resorts.

The solution to the crossword puzzle appears at the back of the magazine,

but I never look at the answers.

When interest rates fall, the price of stocks will rise.

EXERCISE 3A

Underline the subjects of the following sentences *once* and the verbs *twice*. Some sentences may have more than one subject, more than one verb, or both. Remember to cross out the prepositional phrases first.

1. American women have the right to vote today because of the very hard work and sacrifice of some nineteenth century feminists.

2. A leader in this battle for the rights of women was Susan B. Anthony.

3. Susan Anthony began her life in 1820 in Adams, Massachusetts, as the daughter of a Quaker reformer.

4. At the age of seventeen, Anthony became a rural schoolteacher, and she then began to agitate for women's rights such as coeducational public schools, college admission for women, and equal pay for women teachers.

5. In the 1850s Anthony and her friend Elizabeth Stanton were able to get laws on the books in New York state to guarantee women's rights over their children and over control of property and wages.

6. After the Civil War the federal government gave the vote to freed black men but not to women anywhere in the United States.

7. Anthony believed this was very wrong.

8. The right to vote as the key to all women's rights became the single goal of the remainder of Anthony's life.

9. After 1869 she organized support groups of women and some men, wrote countless pamphlets and articles, and campaigned throughout the United States and Europe for women's *suffrage*, the right to vote.

10. In 1872 Anthony and a group of her women followers went to the polls to test the voting rights of the Fourteenth Amendment to the Constitution.

11. The local authorities arrested Anthony, tried her, found her guilty, and fined her.

12. She refused to pay her fine, fought her case all the way to the Supreme Court, and lost.

13. The men of the United States were not ready to allow women to vote.

14. Anthony battled on for women's suffrage until her death in 1906.

15. Fourteen years later in 1920, the Nineteenth Amendment to the Constitution became the law of the land.

16. It granted equal voting rights to women.

17. Today the needs and concerns of women are an essential part of most political campaigns.

EXERCISE 3B

Underline the subjects of the following sentences *once* and the verbs *twice*. Some sentences may have more than one subject, more than one verb, or both. Remember to cross out the prepositional phrases first.

1. Most employees in America enjoy "fringe benefits."

2. Fringe benefits are non-wage compensations to employees.

3. Such benefits to employees include pension plans, holidays, vacation pay, and company-paid programs for life, health, and unemployment insurance.

4. Fringe benefits sometimes come from state legislation.

5. Sometimes employers on their own initiative grant these benefits.

6. And sometimes only strenuous negotiations by unions win fringe benefits for their members.

7. Employers and employees like tax advantages of fringe benefits.

8. The employer pays no tax on the expenses for fringe benefits.

9. The employee pays no tax on this form of compensation either.

10. Because fringe benefits are not taxed, every dollar of benefits goes directly to the employee.

11. An employer also gets much lower insurance rates for the large groups of the employees.

12. The number of fringe benefit programs began to grow sharply during World War II.

13. This growth happened because the government at that time controlled wages severely but not other forms of employee compensation.

14. Recent developments in fringe benefit programs include guaranteed annual wages, bonus payments, and profit-sharing programs.

15. Most employers and most employees like fringe benefits.

EXERCISE 3C

Part One   A prepositional phrase adds more meaning to a sentence, but it also adds a noun or pronoun that may be mistaken for the subject. In each of the following sentences, underline the subject of the sentence *once* and the verb *twice*. Then *add* a prepositional phrase *between* the subject and verb. Does the subject change? The first sentence has been done as an example.

                    to town
1. The <u>bus</u> ∧ <u>left</u> late.

2. The girl smiled at me.

3. The Spanish textbook costs too much.

4. The best program failed to get high ratings.

5. The first few minutes were disappointing.

6. Donna's collection won first prize.

7. The answers were all correct.

8. Her knowledge amazes her friends.

9. The youngest player scored the most points.

10. Jerry's uncle sent him two packages.

Part Two   A preposition is always followed by its object, though it may not be the very next word. In each of the following sentences a preposition is missing its object. Put in a noun or a pronoun for the missing object. Then underline the subject of the sentence *once* and the verb *twice*. The first sentence has been done as an example.

                girls
11. <u>Three</u> of the ∧ <u>left</u> early.

12. Linda's best friend in that moved away to find a new job.

13. The original recipe for the calls for lemon juice.

14. Soon the light of the brightest star in the was visible.

15. The club's president for this brought the meeting to order.

16. Her trip to her father's took five hours.

17. All of the younger players on the got a chance to play.

18. Tonight our ideas about the solution to the puzzling had an audience.

19. The wait for wasn't easy.

20. The location of the store downtown on a busy guaranteed lots of business.

4

Main Verbs
and Helping Verbs

Verbs can be either **main verbs** or **helping** (also called **auxiliary**) **verbs.** Main verbs are the kind of verb you have already studied. Main verbs tell what action is being performed in a sentence. For example:

I *lost* my wallet.
The loud noise *frightened* us.

Helping verbs are used in combination with main verbs. They perform two major functions:

1. Helping verbs indicate shades of meaning that cannot be expressed by a main verb alone. Consider the differences in meaning in the following sentences, in which the helping verbs have been italicized.

I *may* quit my job soon.
I *must* quit my job soon.
I *should* quit my job soon.
I *can* quit my job soon.

As you can see, changing the helping verb changes the meaning of the entire sentence. These differences in meaning could not be expressed simply by using the main verb *quit* alone.

2. Helping verbs also show tense – the time at which the action of the verb takes place. Notice how changing the helping verb in the following sentences helps to change the tense of the main verb *watch*. (Both the helping and the main verbs have been italicized.)

The children *are watching* television now.
The children *will watch* television after dinner.
The children *have watched* television all evening.

Notice the position that helping verbs have in a sentence. They always *come before* the main verb, although sometimes another word, such as an adverb, may come between the helping verb and the main verb.

He *should buy* some life insurance.
He *should* probably *buy* some life insurance.
You *can lose* weight on this diet.
You *can* easily *lose* weight on this diet.

If a question contains a helping verb, the helping verb still *comes before* the main verb.

Will Congress *raise* taxes?
Can we *get* to the airport on time?
Do you *speak* Spanish?
Is the baby *sleeping* now?

The following words are helping verbs. *Memorize them.*

can, could
may, might, must
shall, should
will, would

The following words can be used either as helping verbs or as main verbs.

They are helping verbs if they are used in combination with a main verb. They are main verbs if they occur alone. *Memorize them.*

has, have, had	(forms of the verb *have*)
does, do, did, done	(forms of the verb *do*)
am, is, are, was, were, been	(forms of the verb *be*)

As Main Verbs	*As Helping Verbs*
I *have* two children.	I *have studied* French.
We *did* the assignment.	We *did* not *eat* breakfast.
She *is* here now.	She *is sleeping* now.

From now on, whenever you are asked to identify the verbs in a sentence, *include all the main verbs and all the helping verbs.* For example, in the sentence "We should review this lesson," the complete verb is "should review." In the sentence "He has lost his wallet," the verb is "has lost." Underline the complete verbs in the following sentences.

The team must win tomorrow's game.

Gail may marry Steve next year.

Children often do not like vegetables.

The class has already begun.

Some sentences may contain more than one helping verb.

one helping verb	The landlord *will increase* our rent.
two helping verbs	The plane *should be arriving* soon.
three helping verbs	The new highway *must have been completed* by now.

Underline the subjects of the following sentences *once* and the complete verbs *twice*.

The stores should be closing soon.

Did the sweater fit you?

Your friends must have been joking.

The children had borrowed books from the library.

Would you help me with this exercise?

I will go to the party if you can come with me.

Remember this rule:

The verbs in a sentence include all the main verbs plus all the help-ing verbs.

EXERCISE 4A

Underline the subjects of the following sentence *once* and the complete verbs *twice*. Some sentences may have more than one subject, more than one set of verbs, or both. Remember to cross out prepositional phrases first.

1. Knowledge of the causes of diseases helps medical scientists to discover cures.

2. The causes for many diseases are found in the environment of the victim, but other diseases can be traced to the victim's heredity.

3. In recent years a surprising number of diseases have been found to have hereditary causes.

4. New studies have revealed unexpected reasons for the cause of middle ear infections.

5. These infections are found in many children and result in severe pain and often in temporary hearing loss.

6. They occur when bacteria from the nose and throat migrate to the inner ear.

7. One new study has discovered a hereditary cause for these infections in children of European ancestry.

8. Researchers from the Minnesota Ear, Head and Neck Clinic have studied 249 children on Easter Island in the Pacific Ocean.

9. Though this island is very isolated, some of its children have European ancestors.

10. Easter Island children with European ancestry have many ear infections, but the purely native children are discovered to have none.

11. Ten percent of the children with a mixed heritage and eleven percent of those with a pure European heritage have middle ear infections.

12. All of the children were of the *same* socio-economic status, had the *same* doctor and *same* hospital, and experienced the *same* weather.

13. The results of the Easter Island study are supported by other studies of lower rates of ear infections in black, Hispanic, and Native American children.

14. With this knowledge of a hereditary tendency for these infections, researchers are now directing their attention at a way to prevent them.

EXERCISE 4B

Underline the subjects of the following sentences *once* and the complete verbs *twice*. Some sentences may have more than one subject, more than one set of verbs, or both. Remember to cross out prepositional phrases first.

1. Tony and Michael had been best friends since the first grade.

2. In junior high they took most of the same classes and played together on the football team.

3. Tony played end, and Michael was a winning quarterback.

4. Their senior year of high school should have been their best year as friends, but it wasn't.

5. While Tony was standing in the cafeteria line, he met a girl from his history class.

6. Her name was Isabel, and her beauty was irresistible.

7. Soon Tony was spending all his spare time with the lovely Isabel.

8. Michael was determined not to lose his friendship with Tony.

9. His determination melted away when the football coach asked Tony to switch from end to quarterback.

10. The coach had noticed Tony's passing ability and had decided to try him as first-string quarterback.

11. Michael did not like to be around Tony anymore, and he couldn't stand Isabel.

12. But she surprised him one day by sitting alone with him and talking to him in her usual sultry fashion.

13. She surprised him even more when she agreed to go to the next dance with him.

14. Michael and Isabel were having a great time at the dance, but Tony was miserable.

15. The two old friends would have gotten into a fight if Isabel had not begun to dance with another man at the dance.

16. Tony and Michael asked someone about Isabel's new dance partner.

17. He was a junior in college and played basketball and danced like Gregory Hines!

18. Then she shook them up at intermission with some cold words.

19. "I've outgrown you boys, so now you can be old friends again!"

20. And they were until a new girl arrived at school.

21. She was "just crazy" about football players, especially quarterbacks.

EXERCISE 4C

Part One Construct sentences of your own using the helping verbs listed below.

1. can: _____

_____

2. must: _____

_____

3. will: _____

_____

4. should: _____

_____

5. has: _____

_____

6. was: _____

_____

Part Two Construct a sentence for each of the following patterns. Make certain that the order of the subjects and verbs in your sentences is the same as the order in the pattern. Use as many different helping and main verbs as possible.

S = subject   HV = helping verb   MV = main verb

7. S-MV:

8. S-MV-MV:

9. S-HV-MV:

10. S-HV-HV-MV:

11. S-HV-HV-HV-MV:

12. HV-S-MV?: (Notice that this pattern produces a question, not a statement.)

5

The Position of Verbals

In some languages the reader can always tell whether a word is a noun or verb or some other part of speech by just looking at the word. This is true of some words in English, but in most cases we have to see how a particular word fits into a sentence pattern before we can call it a "noun" or a "verb." Look at the word *trains* in these two sentences:

My brother trains horses for a living.
The trains rolled down the track.

Trains is a verb in the first sentence because it comes in a **verb position** in the sentence pattern. But in the second sentence *trains* is a noun because it comes in a **subject position.** The position of words is very important in English grammar. Saying that "John shot George" is very different from saying "George shot John." Some words in our language will shift into three or even four positions:

The people in that church *fast* during Lent.   (verb position)
Tony's *fast* took off five pounds.   (noun position)

The *fast* car had engine trouble.   (adjective position)

Eileen can run *fast*.   (adverb position)

This question of position in the sentence pattern is very important in seeing how one special group of words — **verbals** — plays a part in identifying subjects and verbs. **Verbals** are forms of verbs that, when placed in certain positions in the sentence pattern, will act like nouns or adjectives. Because verbals are closely related to verbs, you need to recognize them when you see them and not to confuse them with verbs. Verbals are **gerunds, participles,** or **infinitives.** Look at these sentences:

The man was *running*. (*running* in verb position = **main verb**)
Running was his hobby. (*running* in subject position = **gerund**)
The *running* man fell down. (*running* in adjective position = **participle**)
To run for a medal is his dream. (*To run* in subject position = **infinitive**)

Nouns (*car, pizza, Carla Smith*) and subject pronouns (*they, we, she*) are the most common subjects. But gerunds (*running, thinking, eating*) are also commonly used for subjects ("*Running* is her hobby"). Infinitives (*to run, to eat, to think*) are sometimes used as subjects also ("*To run* through the park is her favorite pastime"). To practice this, put first a noun, then a gerund, and then an infinitive in the three subject positions below:

_____ is not always easy. (Start with "The . . .")

_____ is not always easy.

_____ is not always easy.

Since gerunds and participles look alike because they both end in –*ing* ("The *rinsing* took twenty seconds" or "The *rinsing* solution came in a bottle"), the only way you can tell them apart is by their position in the sentence pattern. In these sentences, which are gerunds (subjects), and which are participles (modifiers of nouns)?

The washing machine is new.
The washing should take about five minutes.
Earning money gives a person self-respect.
Her earning power was reduced after her accident.

Notice that gerunds, like nouns, may be modified by adjectives and prepositional phrases:

The first *running* of the race was in July, 1988.
The sudden and fierce *rushing* of the wind blew over the shack.

Gerunds may also act like nouns in other ways. They may be objects or objects of prepositions. Again, the way you can tell the difference between the verb and the verbal is by position in the sentence pattern:

John is *running* the race again. (*running* as part of verb)
The thought of *running* again made him tired. (as object of preposition)
Sandra likes *running*. (as object of verb)

Notice that you would still have good sentences if you substituted nouns for the two gerunds.

The participles that we have looked at so far have all ended in *-ing*. These are called **present participles** because they come from verbs in the present tense ("The car is *rolling*"). When participles come from verbs in the past tense, they are called **past participles** ("The player was *injured*"). Past participles are also commonly used to modify subjects. Again you should notice the position of the participle before you decide whether it is being used as part of the verb or being used to modify a subject.

The player was *injured* badly.
The *injured* player left the game.
The students were *tired* by all the homework.
The *tired* students fell asleep.

Below is a group of sentences. Of course, they will all have verbs. But they will also include these **verbals**: gerunds as subjects, gerunds as objects of prepositions, gerunds as objects of verbs, infinitives as subjects, present participles as modifiers of nouns, and past participles as modifiers of nouns. First mark the *verbs* in the sentences. Then using the location of the verbal as your main clue, circle each *verbal* and label it as a "gerund" or "infinitive" or "participle." The first sentence has been done as an example:

gerund
v
Her (winning) made us extremely happy.

The losing team left the court first.

The cost of painting surprised us.

To get high grades is not easy for everyone.

The paved road was shown in red.

The neglected road was paved by the city.

Her divorced parents are going to remarry.

Leaving this job would hurt my pocketbook.

The racing car flew off the track.

EXERCISE 5A

Underline the subjects of the following sentences *once* and the verbs *twice*. Remember that *gerunds*, as well as nouns and pronouns, can be subjects.

1. Because folk medicine is not an exact science, people have often ridiculed folk remedies.

2. Taking the plant *meadow saffron* for gout has been considered one of those doubtful ''cures.''

3. Now, that particular folk remedy is getting the approval of medical scientists.

4. Drinking *meadow saffron* ''tea'' has been helping gout sufferers for centuries.

5. Recently scientists have extracted the useful part of the plant and have named the new drug *colchicine*.

6. Certain processes in the cell lead to gout, and colchicine seems to interfere with these processes.

7. Today researchers hope to use colchicine on a much more serious disease, *multiple sclerosis*.

8. This disease attacks the central nervous system and usually leads to vision problems, muscular weakness, or spasticity.

9. Colchicine studies have been conducted recently with mice and with volunteer victims of multiple sclerosis.

10. The researchers are hoping to see colchicine attack certain specialized cells.

11. These cells are always present when multiple sclerosis begins to develop.

12. The studies look very promising, but expanding them is proving to be difficult because of the competition for research dollars.

13. Today over 250,000 people in the United States have multiple sclerosis.

14. None of the current treatments are satisfactory because all of them have very toxic side effects.

15. Although many old folk remedies have been shown by science to be only superstitions, perhaps *meadow saffron* will prove to be a cure for the difficult disease of multiple sclerosis.

EXERCISE 5B

Underline the subjects of the following sentences *once* and the complete verbs *twice*. Remember that gerunds and infinitives, as well as nouns and pronouns, may be subjects. Also remember that participles, like adjectives, may modify nouns.

1. Love is blind.

2. Speak softly and carry a big stick.

3. A watched pot never boils.

4. Actions speak louder than words.

5. You can't fit a round peg in a square hole.

6. Washing a cat wastes time and soap.

7. A soft answer turns away wrath.

8. Too many cooks spoil the broth.

9. A rolling stone gathers no moss.

10. A bird in the hand is worth two in the bush.

11. The road to hell is paved with good intentions.

12. Power tends to corrupt, and absolute power tends to corrupt absolutely.

13. Well begun is half done.

14. Time waits for no man.

15. Success breeds success.

16. An apple a day keeps the doctor away.

17. Birds of a feather flock together.

18. Seeing is believing.

19. Do not throw pearls before swine.

20. You can't unscramble an egg.

21. Hope springs eternal in the human breast.

(What kinds of words are missing, though understood, in the next two sentences?)

22. To err is human, to forgive divine.

23. No pain, no gain.

EXERCISE 5C

This exercise gives you practice in changing the location of verbals to give them a different job in the sentence.

Part One For the sentences below, underline the subjects *once* and the verbs *twice*. Then below each sentence write a second sentence in which you change the *–ing* part of the verb into a **gerund** subject by moving it into the subject position. The second sentence does not have to have the same meaning as the first sentence. After you finish your new sentence, underline its subject and verb. The first pair has been done as an example.

1. The girl is running through the obstacle course.

   Running through the obstacle course takes much energy.

2. The woman is learning quickly.

   _____

3. The President is speaking on television.

   _____

4. Marie has been getting up at 5:00 A.M.

   _____

5. Julie was leaving college reluctantly.

   _____

6. Professor Johnson is expecting lots of homework.

   _____

7. The semester will be ending on June 10th.

   _____

Part Two This part is about moving the location of the participle to change it from the main verb to a modifier of the subject. For the sentence below mark subjects and verbs as usual. Then make up a second sentence which uses the present or past participle of the verb as a participle modifying a subject. Circle your new modifier. *The second sentence does not have to have the same meaning as the first sentence.* Item number 8 has been done as an example.

8. The old <u>man</u> <u>was tired</u> from the work.

The (tired) old man went to bed.

9. The fish was swimming through the water.

10. The house was painted last year.

11. That contestant is winning the big prize.

12. The current was moving swiftly toward the shore.

13. These values have been treasured through the centuries.

Subject-Verb Identification
Unit Review

Underline the subjects of the following sentences *once* and the complete verbs *twice*. Some sentences have more than one subject, more than one verb, or both.

A monument to a person should symbolize that person. The Washington Monument in our nation's capital symbolizes the simple strength of George Washington and the beauty of his life.

In shape the monument is a tall four-sided spire. This shape is called an *obelisk*. It was used first by the ancient Egyptians. The square base of the monument measures 55 feet on each side. From this square base the structure tapers 555 feet to its top. These proportions are identical to those of the Egyptian original.

The hollow core of the monument is constructed of granite from the Sierra mountain range of California. This granite core is faced with white Maryland marble over the entire exterior surface. The shaft weighs 91,000 tons, and it is regarded by engineers as one of the world's most remarkable masonry structures.

The setting of the monument enhances its effect on the viewer. It stands alone in over 100 acres of parklike grounds. The Capitol Building and the Mall lie well to the east. At some distance to the west lie the Reflecting Pool and the Lincoln Memorial.

If you are visiting Washington, step outdoors after sunset. At night the plain white shaft is floodlit from its base to its tip. It can be seen for many miles in every direction. Its strength and austere beauty speak well of the first president.

SUBJECT–VERB AGREEMENT

6

Recognizing Singular and Plural Subjects and Verbs

Errors in **subject–verb agreement** are among the most common grammatical mistakes. By applying the rules in this unit, you should be able to correct many of the errors in your own writing.

As you already know, a sentence must contain both a subject and a verb. Read the following two sentences. What is the grammatical difference between them?

> The restaurant opens at noon.
> The restaurants open at noon.

In the first sentence, the subject *restaurant* is singular. **Singular** means "one." There is only *one* restaurant in the first sentence. In the second sentence, the subject *restaurants* is plural. **Plural** means "two or more." There are at least two (and possibly more than two) restaurants in the second sentence.

Like the subject *restaurant*, the verb *opens* in the first sentence is singular. Verb forms ending in *s* are used with *singular* subjects, as in the sentence "The restaurant accepts credit cards.'' The verb *open* in the second sentence above is **plural.** This verb form (without a final *s*) is used with *plural* subjects, as in the sentence ''The restaurants accept credit cards.''

In other words, if the subject of a sentence is *singular*, the verb in the sentence must also be *singular*. If the subject of the sentence is *plural*, the verb must be *plural*. This matching of singular subjects with singular verbs and plural subjects with plural verbs is called **subject–verb agreement.**

In order to avoid making mistakes in subject–verb agreement, you must be able to recognize the difference between singular and plural subjects and verbs.

The subjects of sentences are usually nouns or pronouns. As you know, the plurals of nouns are usually formed by adding an *s* to singular forms.

Singular	*Plural*
envelope	envelopes
restaurant	restaurants

However, a few nouns (under 1 percent) have irregular plural forms.

Singular	*Plural*
man	men
child	children
knife	knives
thesis	theses
medium	media (as in the ''mass media'')

Those pronouns that can be used as subjects are also singular or plural, depending upon whether they refer to one or to more than one person or thing.

Singular	*Plural*
I	we
you	you
he, she, it	they

Notice that the pronoun *you* may be either singular or plural.

If nouns show number by adding *s* to the plural, what do verbs do to show whether they are singular or plural? A long time ago English verbs had many different endings for this purpose, but most of those endings have been dropped. Today most English verbs look the same whether the subject is singular or plural: "I see," "we see," "the boys see," "I jumped," "they jumped," "the frogs jumped," and so on. However, there is one place where English verbs have kept a special ending to show number. That special ending is also an *s*, and the only place it is added is the **present tense singular** with the subject pronouns *he, she, it,* and with any singular noun that could replace *it.* Look at these sentences in the present tense and notice when the *s* comes on the verb:

Singular	*Plural*
I see.	We see.
You see.	You see.
He sees.	They see.
She sees.	They see.
It sees.	They see.
The boy sees.	They see.
The girl sees.	They see.
The cat sees.	They see.
One nurse cares for him.	Three nurses care for him.

To sum up, although adding an *s* to most nouns (99 percent) makes them plural, some singular verbs also end with an *s.* An easy way to remember this difference is to memorize this rule:

Any verb ending in s is singular.

There are no exceptions to this rule. Therefore, it is not **good usage** in college writing to have a sentence in which a plural subject is matched with a verb ending in *s.* Effective writers are as aware of **usage** as they are of grammar.

Good usage means choosing different kinds of language for different situations, just as we choose different clothes for different situations. In **informal** situations, such as conversations with friends, it is common to choose informal usage. However, almost all of the writing you do for college is in **formal** situations, such as exams and essay assignments. The difference between formal and informal usage can be seen when we make subjects agree with their verbs. Because most conversation is very informal, you may have heard or have used many informal verb choices in your own conversations. Notice the differences in usage in these examples:

Informal	*Formal*
We was good friends.	We were good friends.
That don't sound right.	That doesn't sound right.
They was angry with the decision.	They were angry with the decision.

You want your college writing to be as effective as you can make it. In college you must choose **formal usage** in almost every situation—essays, reports, exams and so on. The exercises in our text are *always* designed for you to choose formal usage.

In order to avoid subject–verb agreement errors, there are some rules that you should keep in mind. (How you "keep rules in mind" is up to you. If you find that even after you study rules, you still cannot remember them, you should memorize the rules in this unit.)

Rule 1. A verb agrees with the subject, not with the complement. A **complement** is a word that refers to the same person or thing as the subject of the sentence. It follows a linking verb.

      S   LV   C
Our main *problem is* high prices.

In the sentence above, the subject is *problem*, which is singular. The subject is not *prices*. Rather, *prices* is the complement. Therefore, the linking verb takes the singular form *is* to agree with *problem*. If the sentence is reversed, it reads:

      S   LV   C
High *prices are* our main problem.

The subject is now the plural noun *prices*, and *problem* is the complement. The verb now takes the plural form *are*. Which are the correct verbs in the following sentences?

The topic of conversation (was, were) the latest movies.
Beans (is, are) the main ingredient in this recipe.

Rule 2. Do not mistakenly make your verb agree with a noun or pronoun in a prepositional phrase. (This is easy to do because many prepositional phrases come just before a verb.)

A *woman* with four children *lives* in that house.

In the sentence above, the subject is singular (*woman*). The prepositional phrase *with four children* has no effect on the verb, which remains singular (*lives*).

One of the colleges has a soccer team.

The singular verb *has* agrees with the singular subject *one*, not with the plural object of the preposition (*colleges*).

Which are the correct verbs in the following sentences?

The length of women's skirts (seems, seem) to change every year.
The cause of his many successes (are, is) obvious.

Rule 3. Be especially alert for subject–verb agreement when the sentence has **inverted word order** as in these three situations:

a) **questions**

Notice the location of the subject in these questions:

HV   S   MV
Do they like that class? (subject between helping and main verb)

V   S
Is Reynaldo your best friend? (subject after helping and main verb)

Interrogative words like *when, where,* and *how* come at the beginning of sentence patterns, but they are never subjects.

       HV   S   MV
When *does* your *bus leave*? (subject between helping and main verb)

       V   S
Where *are* her *books*? (subject after verb)

     HV S   MV
How *did he make* the team? (subject between helping and main verb)

b) **sentence patterns beginning with *here* or *there***

Notice the location of the subject in these patterns:

There *are* fifty *states* in the United States. (subject after verb)
Here *is* your old chemistry *notebook*. (subject after verb)

The words *here* or *there* are never subjects.

c) **rare patterns in which the verb precedes the subject**

Occasionally a writer will, for emphasis, put a subject after its verb. Notice the location of the subject in these sentences:

Among his most valuable possessions *is* an antique *car*. (If the order of this sentence were reversed, it would read, "An antique *car is* among his most valuable possessions.")

In the middle of the wall *hang* two large *paintings*. ("Two large *paintings hang* in the middle of the wall.")

EXERCISE 6A

Circle the verb that correctly completes each sentence. Choose formal usage. Make certain that you have identified the correct subject of the sentence and that you have crossed out prepositional phrases.

1. During the Vietnam War, Admiral Elmo Zumwalt (was, were) commanding a special group of sailors in small boats.

2. These boats (was, were) called "brown-water" units because they patrolled the muddy rivers of South Vietnam.

3. Under Admiral Zumwalt's command (was, were) his own son Lieutenant Elmo Zumwalt, III.

4. The brown-water casualty rates (were, was) running at seventy percent.

5. The most dangerous enemy for Zumwalt's patrol boats (were, was) the snipers in the bushes near the rivers.

6. Admiral Zumwalt decided to use a chemical defoliant to strip the snipers' cover in the vegetation along the river bank.

7. The chosen defoliant (were, was) called Agent Orange.

8. Though its side-effects on the human body (was, were) not fully understood, Agent Orange was a proven defoliant in the United States.

9. American planes dropped Agent Orange along the riverbanks, and soon the foliage there (was, were) dying.

10. As the snipers lost their cover, the weekly casualty rates in Zumwalt's command (were, was) dropping rapidly.

11. By the time all the foliage (were, was) gone, the rate was down to less than one percent.

12. The jungle hideouts of the enemy had been eliminated, and United States ships under Zumwalt (were, was) able to patrol with little fear of snipers.

13. Several years after returning home, Admiral Zumwalt's son became ill with Hodgkin's disease and lymphoma.

14. By this time, there (was, were) clear links between these forms of cancer and Agent Orange.

15. Young Zumwalt fought the disease bravely for many years while researchers (were, was) struggling to find a remedy.

16. He died in the summer of 1988 at the age of 42.

17. What (has, have) been the Zumwalts' feelings about Agent Orange?

18. Because so many combat sailors lives (was, were) saved, Zumwalt and his son believed completely in the *rightness* of the Admiral's decision to defoliate the hideouts with Agent Orange.

19. Today the Admiral's grandson (are, is) suffering from a severe learning disability.

20. These same side-effects from Agent Orange (has, have) been turning up in many Vietnam veterans and their children and also in many families in South Vietnam.

EXERCISE 6B

Some of the sentences in this exercise contain subject–verb agreement errors. Others are correct as written. If the sentence contains a subject–verb agreement error, cross out the incorrect verb, and write the correct verb in its place. If the sentence is correct, write a *C* in the margin by the sentence number.

1. There seem to be no limit to the ways humans have found to decorate their faces.

2. Wall paintings of Egyptians' faces from five thousand years ago reveal the use of eye shadow and of shaped eyebrows.

3. The aborigines of Australia has decorated their faces in traditional designs for many thousands of years.

4. On the faces of American Indian warriors were painted bright stripes of war paint.

5. Would you smear a paste of fresh bacon grease and egg white on your face?

6. That paste was used by ladies of seventeenth century England to achieve a chic, white look.

7. Both sexes at that time was known to use false eyebrows of mouse hair and wigs of horses' tails.

8. During this period many faces was ravaged with disease and malnutrition, and so powders and rouge helped disguise these facial disfigurements.

9. How was these people to know about the poisonous lead and other dangerous ingredients in their cosmetics?

10. Another cosmetic device in these times were to disguise smallpox scars with small hearts, moons, or stars of black silk.

11. There was a gradual decline in the use of cosmetic pastes and powders in the nineteenth century as health improved and as soap and water were used to bring out a natural look.

12. Today males in our culture has almost given up any artificial decoration of the face.

13. But for most of today's females cosmetics seems to be a necessity.

14. On the face of the contemporary woman appears the products of a multi-million-dollar industry in the form of eye lashes, eye shadow, mascara, rouge, skin creams and toners, lipstick, and, lately, cosmetic contact lenses.

15. Will our great-great-grandchildren think of *us* as very strange creatures?

EXERCISE 6C

In the following sentences change each plural subject to its singular form and change each subject to its plural form. As you change each subject, change its verb to agree with it. The first sentence has been done as an example.

      sisters like
1. My ~~sister~~ ~~likes~~ ice cream.

2. Is your sister here?

3. The teenager with dark glasses was seen by a witness.

4. There is a good reason to buy early.

5. His cars use a lot of gas.

6. The solutions of the chairman require higher standards.

7. The dress with the bright colors makes her look happier.

8. Among those candidates is the new leader.

9. Her main reason for a visit was her sister's recipes.

10. The car's color shines at night.

11. The unhappy result of the party was hangovers.

12. The desserts at the dinner are colorfully decorated.

13. How have your sisters been getting along?

14. The lady in the rear wants you to speak louder.

15. Here is the answer to your problems.

16. The reasons for Ramon's sudden interest in her are not clear.

17. Lila's recipe looks like a gourmet's.

18. The leaders of the team run out on the field first.

19. In the corner sits the trophy from our best season.

7

Indefinite Pronouns as Subjects

The subject pronouns we have been studying, like *she* or *it* or *they*, refer to specific, definite persons or things. This chapter is about another kind of pronoun, **indefinite pronouns,** which do not refer to a specific person or to definite things.

Rule 4. The following indefinite pronouns are singular and require singular verbs:

anybody, anyone, anything
each, each one
either, neither
everybody, everyone, everything
nobody, no one, nothing
somebody, someone, something

Everybody likes you.
Does everyone need a ticket?

Each of these jobs *pays* the minimum wage.
Either of those times *is* all right with me.

Notice that in the last two sentences, the verbs agree with the singular subjects *each* and *either*. The verbs are not affected by the plural nouns in the prepositional phrases *of these jobs* or *of those times*.

Rule 5.   **Indefinite pronouns,** such as the words *some, half, most,* and *all,* may take either singular or plural verbs, depending upon their meaning in the context of the sentence. If these words tell **how much** of something is meant, the verb is singular; but if they tell **how many** of something is meant, the verb is plural.

Most of the milk *is* sour. (how much?)
These oranges look good, but *most* of them *are* sour. (how many?)
Some of the land *contains* gold. (how much?)
Some of the boxes *contain* money. (how many?)
All of the hospital *has* air conditioning. (how much?)
All of my children *have* the flu. (how many?)

(Do not confuse the words in this rule with the words *each, either,* and *neither* in Rule 4. These three words always require a singular verb.)

EXERCISE 7A

Circle the verb that correctly completes each sentence. Choose formal usage.

1. Everybody with a pass (get, gets) in free.

2. Anything over ten dollars (needs, need) a receipt.

3. The effect of her words (were, was) electric.

4. When (does, do) the early editions of the paper go on sale?

5. Many of the older students (are, is) taking that course.

6. There (is, are) some very good reasons to major in engineering.

7. This week's lectures (is, are) all free.

8. In the middle of the campus (stand, stands) seven oak trees.

9. Someone from the Virgin Islands (are, is) speaking at 11:00.

10. Most of the cheese from the surplus (was, were) given to the poor.

11. (Do, Does) either of these candidates represent your views?

12. Almost all of Lisa's qualifications (meets, meet) the requirements.

13. The price of tickets (have, has) gone up.

14. New solutions (are, is) the answer to the problem.

15. Anyone with those characteristics (is, are) going to do a good job.

16. A few of the faster runners (were, was) able to lap the field.

17. There (are, is) surely someone in those clubs to lead the council.

18. The goal of her teams (is, are) always victory.

19. How (do, does) the doctor's nurses keep so many patients happy?

20. In the center of the plaza (plays, play) the joyful children.

EXERCISE 7B

Some of the sentences in this exercise contain subject–verb agreement errors. Others are correct as written. If the sentence contains a subject–verb agreement error, cross out the incorrect verb and write the correct verb in its place. If the sentence is correct, write a *C* in the margin by the sentence number.

1. Many of the girls left early.

2. Someone always leave her books on my desk.

3. Each of John's pencils are sharpened.

4. How is each of the girls going to know the time for her appointment?

5. Everybody with tickets get a rain check.

6. Most of the milk have turned bad.

7. A yard with lots of flowerbeds need much more care.

8. Do either of you know the way to Jenny's house?

9. The difficulty with Tony's designs are the lines near the top.

10. All of the building have forced-air heating.

11. His main goal for now are answers to the questions.

12. Anything on that table sells for half price.

13. The appearance of these older models with tail fins appeal to many car buffs.

14. One of Lila's friends insist on her innocence.

15. Something like those earrings with pearls were on sale.

16. There's several ways to do this problem.

17. How do these people survive?

18. The costs for each item are shown in this chart.

19. Her reward to him is three home-cooked meals.

20. Some of the pages in my anthropology text is missing.

EXERCISE 7C

In the following sentences change all singular subjects to their plural form and all plural subjects to their singular form. If these changes affect subject–verb agreement, then change the verb to match the new subject. The first sentence has been done as an example.

       problems   were

1. The ~~problem~~ with the neighbors ~~was~~ their dogs.

2. The boys were welcome.

3. The answers to the question were a surprise.

4. The owner's response to a long survey about products was good.

5. The reasons for her answer were not clear.

6. Do your sister and brother like parties?

7. The old man and the kittens were playing in the yard.

8. The treasure in all those wooden chests is rubies, pearls and gold.

9. His great victory comes at the end of the season.

10. There is no clear set of prints for these negatives.

11. People with pets are not permitted.

12. The result of the contest was three prizes.

13. The girl in the green, blue, and silver uniform was the best.

14. The recipe consists of eggs, flour, sugar, and milk.

15. What does the employee know about meeting a payroll?

16. Have your friends been through orientation?

17. In the museum hangs Picasso's best-known painting.

18. Here is the answer for that problem.

8

Subjects Understood in a Special Sense

This chapter discusses as subjects several small groups of words that call for special attention in subject–verb agreement.

Rule 6. Some subjects, though **plural in form,** are **singular in meaning** and therefore require a singular verb. Such words include *news, mathematics, physics, economics, mumps,* and *measles.*

Mathematics is required for engineering majors.
Mumps makes it difficult to swallow.

Rule 7. A **unit of time, weight, measurement,** or **money** usually requires a singular verb because the entire amount is thought of as a single unit.

Two *hours was* not long enough for that test.
Fifty *dollars seems* a reasonable price for that jacket.
Four *ounces* of chocolate *is* needed for this recipe.

Rule 8. **Collective nouns** usually require singular verbs. A collective noun is a word that is singular in form but that refers to a group of people or things. Some common collective nouns are words such as *group, team, family, class, crowd,* and *committee.*

The *team practices* every afternoon.
The *crowd has been* very noisy.

Occasionally, a collective noun may be used with a plural verb if the writer wishes to show that the members of the group are acting as separate individuals rather than as a unified body. Notice the difference in meaning between the following pair of sentences:

The City Council has agreed to raise taxes. (In this sentence, *the City Council* is acting as a single, unified group.)

The City Council are arguing over a proposal to raise taxes. (In this sentence, *the City Council* is viewed as a collection of separate individuals who, because they are not in agreement, are not acting as a unified group.)

EXERCISE 8A

Circle the verb that correctly completes each sentence. Choose formal usage.

1. Around their roof (was, were) strings of Christmas lights.

2. Their committee (meet, meets) on Monday.

3. (Do, Does) your team want to leave early?

4. The all-star team (consist, consists) of the best players from the whole county.

5. A group of forty people (is, are) going.

6. Three quarts of juice (adds, add) flavor to the punch.

7. There (is, are) at least two good reasons for voting yes.

8. Two ounces in each cup (were, was) more than enough.

9. How (have, has) the board reached its decision?

10. Mumps usually (last, lasts) about ten days to two weeks.

11. Twenty cents (were, was) not enough for the bus fare.

12. Here (are, is) the corrected problems for the homework.

13. Among the happy victors (was, were) a surprisingly sad face.

14. The City Council (argues, argue) violently sometimes.

15. Economics (are, is) on the schedule of all of the business majors.

16. Many of the counselors for this major (is, are) also teachers.

17. Everyone in the class (is, are) going on the field trip.

18. (Has, Have) the jury on his case reached a verdict?

19. The training exercises (last, lasts) for two weeks.

EXERCISE 8B

Some of the sentences in this exercise contain subject–verb agreement errors. Others are correct as written. If the sentence contains a subject–verb agreement error, cross out the incorrect verb, and write the correct form in its place. If the sentence is correct, write *C* in the margin by the sentence number. This exercise covers rules from Lessons 6–8.

1. *Pack rats* is small rodents.

2. They are noted for collecting bright, shiny objects.

3. Pack rats stores the objects in their nests.

4. No one is sure of the reason for this behavior.

5. Does any of your acquaintances act like the pack rat?

6. According to an article in *Psychology Today* by Lynda Warren and Jonnae Ostrom, many humans exhibits pack-rat behavior.

7. Some people saves all of their junk mail, while others never throws away their daily newspapers.

8. Some human "pack rats" never throw away any receipts or business memos.

9. Even when there is some real value to the pack rats' objects, like lumber or fabric remnants, why will they never use the saved items or often save more than a lifetime's supply?

10. Unlike the systematic and catalogued collection of an ordinary "collector," the stockpile of pack rats are usually just that, a pile, and they feel no need to display or organize their hoards of objects.

11. Most of us associates pack-rat behavior with older people and assume that the behavior show a fear of the future.

12. But many pack rats are young and well-to-do people.

13. Psychologists are interested in the effect of pack-rat behavior on the people around the pack rat.

14. If your spouse or one of your relatives is a pack rat, you will probably be very aware of it and will probably resent the "irrationality" of the pack rat, not to mention the crowding and clutter from that person's habit.

15. The bad news are that most of us have some pack-rat tendencies.

16. The good news is that it's easier to see pack-rat behavior in other people.

EXERCISE 8C

Some of the sentences in this exercise contain subject–verb agreement errors. Others are correct as written. If the sentence contains a subject–verb agreement error, cross out the incorrect verb, and write the correct form in its place. If the sentence is correct, write *C* in the margin by the sentence number. This exercise covers rules from Lessons 6–8.

1. Most of the pie were eaten.

2. Someone in the afternoon classes is going to win the prize.

3. Here is the answers to your questions.

4. Has her team been told the rules?

5. Four gallons of unleaded gasoline cost almost four dollars.

6. The committee for publications meet every Thursday.

7. Some of those people are my friends.

8. The result of many of Aaron's gambles are victories for the team.

9. Through these doors passes the best cooks in the world.

10. Her economics classes is not exactly easy.

11. Two hours was not enough time to complete that exam.

12. Where was your father's relatives when the game was over?

13. Pat co-exists happily with her cat and dog in a small apartment.

14. Four dollars are about the right price for that item on sale.

15. Good news travel fast.

16. The deer was jumping after one another to get away.

17. The executive committee have fought long and hard about the policy.

18. Do mathematics appeal to you?

9

When Subjects Are
Joined by Conjunctions

Subjects joined by conjunctions require the special rules in this chapter.

Rule 9. Two subjects joined by the conjunction *and* are plural and require a plural verb.

> *Maine* and *Idaho* both *grow* large amounts of potatoes.

Rule 10. When *each, every,* or *any* is used as an adjective in front of subjects, the subjects that are modified require a singular verb. (Writers have the most trouble with this rule when the sentence has two or more subjects joined by *and,* so this rule is an exception to Rule 9 above.)

> *Every* car and motorcycle *needs* license plates.
> *Each* cafe and deli *is inspected* by the Board of Health.

Notice that the adjectives *every* and *each* make the verbs in the sentences singular even though each sentence has more than one subject.

Rule 11. Two singular subjects joined by the conjunctions *or* or *nor* are singular and require a singular verb.

Soup or *salad is included* with your meal.
Neither the *supermarket* nor the *drugstore sells* nails.

Rule 12. If both a singular and a plural subject are joined by *or* or *nor*, the subject that is **closer** to the verb determines whether the verb is singular or plural.

Either *checks* or a credit *card is* acceptable at this hotel.
Either a credit *card* or *checks are* acceptable at this hotel.
Are travelers *checks* or a credit *card accepted* at this hotel?
Is a credit *card* or travelers *checks accepted* at this hotel?

(Note: in the final two sentences it is the *helping* verb that agrees.)

EXERCISE 9A

Circle the verb that correctly completes each sentence.

1. Neither a sore back nor shin splints (interfere, interferes) with her daily run.

2. Smith and Jones (has, have) taken the easy way out.

3. The title of the book and its cover (were, was) eye-catching.

4. Everybody at the game (listen, listens) to the band.

5. Every tailback and halfback (has, have) to practice blocking.

6. Someone with keen perceptions (has, have) made this picture.

7. Either three tickets or enough cash (gets, get) you those seats.

8. Their knowledge of all the circumstances (were, was) doubtful.

9. (Does, Do) each girl and boy in the class know the right answer?

10. Everybody always (wins, win) too easily.

11. Hot dogs and steak (were, was) on the menu.

12. Any bright blue or green (look, looks) attractive on Maria.

13. Neither Gary nor his brothers (is, are) going to the dance.

14. Answers for the solution to all the problems (exists, exist) in the computer's memory.

15. Roses or lilies (look, looks) best in that vase.

16. Either Rosie or Whitney (has, have) won the prize.

17. (Do, Does) the Republicans and the Democrats get equal time?

18. How (has, have) John and the team been getting along?

EXERCISE 9B

Some of the sentences in this exercise contain subject–verb agreement errors. Others are correct as written. If the sentence contains a subject–verb agreement error, cross out the incorrect verb, and write the correct form in its place. If the sentence is correct, write *C* in the margin by the sentence number. This exercise covers rules from Lessons 6–9.

1. The time is March of 1862, and the eleven states of the Southern Confederacy has begun their war to secede from the United States.

2. In the waters off Norfolk, Virginia, a fleet of wooden ships of the Union navy form a blockade to keep valuable supplies from reaching the Southern cities.

3. On March 8 a strange-looking vessel sails eastward directly toward the tall masts and sails of the Union fleet.

4. The strange ship sits very low in the water, and although it has no masts or sails, it move at high speed toward the Union ship *Cumberland* and rams it.

5. The *Cumberland* begins to sink, and the other Confederate ships move to attack the single dark ship.

6. Cannon shells and bullets from the Union ships slams into the strange ship and fall harmlessly into the water.

7. The strange ship runs the Union ship *Congress* aground, destroys it, and then turns on the rest of the Northern fleet.

8. By this time the other ships of the Union fleet has scattered in all directions.

9. Because a whole fleet of wooden sailing ships have just been defeated by a single steam-powered, ironclad vessel, naval warfare will never be the same.

10. That vessel was the former Union steam ship *Merrimack,* and it had been salvaged by Southern engineers after being abandoned by the North.

11. The Southern engineers covered the wooden hull of the *Merrimack* with iron plates and sent it against the Yankees to break their blockade.

12. On March 9 the *Merrimack* again sails out against the Union fleet, but another strange ship await her.

13. The Union admirals have been secretly building their own ironclad ship, the *Monitor,* and it has rushed south to aid in the blockade.

14. For four hours, the *Merrimack* and the *Monitor* fires cannon blast after cannon blast at one another.

15. Neither the multiple guns of the *Merrimack* nor the single huge revolving gun of the *Monitor* damage its opponent.

16. The battle of the ironclads end in a draw, and the two ships never fight again.

17. But now the inventors must get busy, for new weapons of war is needed to meet the threat of ''unsinkable'' ships.

EXERCISE 9C

Some of the sentences in this exercise contain subject–verb agreement errors. Others are correct as written. If a sentence contains a subject–verb agreement error, cross out the incorrect verb and write the correct verb in its place. If a sentence is correct, write a *C* in the margin by the sentence number. This exerise covers rules from Exercises 6–9.

1. Over the roof flew a pale, purple ghost.

2. Their group meets monthly.

3. Does any of you lab assistants want to leave early?

4. The coach and the players cooperates for the good of the team.

5. The varsity team of forty players are going.

6. The cloves of garlic lends a tang to the recipe.

7. There is at least two consequences from his accident.

8. Neither the cayenne pepper nor the five jalapeno chiles makes the dish tasty enough to suit me.

9. Every Republican and Democrat are bound by the new law.

10. Measles is not a disease to be taken lightly.

11. Either the *Angels* or the *Dodgers* are going to win the pennant.

12. Here is the plans for the parade.

13. Hector Alvarez and Alicia Harrison are engaged.

14. The School Board elect a new chairperson tonight.

15. Either Joanie or her children is looking after the cat.

16. How has the executive committee determined the new rule?

17. Among the many flowers were three happy bees.

18. Statistics is on the schedule of all of the psychology majors.

Subject–Verb Agreement
Unit Review

Correct any subject–verb agreement errors that you find in the following essay by crossing out the incorrect verb and writing in the correct form. It may help you to underline all the subjects in the essay *once* and all the verbs *twice* before you try to identify errors in agreement.

Sometimes the contributions of a person to human progress remains unknown until by accident the facts of the case is revealed. For many years the credit for inventing electronic computers were given to the wrong people.

In 1967 the Honeywell Corporation were sued by the Sperry Rand Corporation for refusing to pay royalties on Sperry's ENIAC computer. Up to that time the ENIAC was considered the first electronic computer in the United States. Sperry Rand owned the patent to ENIAC and collected money from other companies for use of its computer or for developing computers like ENIAC. The Honeywell Corporation did not like Sperry Rand's control of all electronic computers. Honeywell countersued Sperry Rand for violating antitrust regulations and for attempting to enforce an invalid patent.

While the lawyers for Honeywell was preparing to fight Sperry Rand, they discovered some very important and interesting information: 1) In the 1930s an unknown professor, John V. Atanasoff at Iowa State College, had worked on a design for electronic computers. 2) Atanasoff had shared his ideas in the early 1940s with John W. Mauchly. 3) Mauchly had built ENIAC in Pennsylvania *after* he had worked with Atanasoff.

In Atanasoff's testimony in the Honeywell case, there was some essential questions for him to answer for the judge: Were he and his collaborator, Clifford Berry, operating a successful electronic computer *before* Mauchly's ENIAC computer began to operate in 1945? Was Mauchly and the other builders of ENIAC using computer principles from the earlier work of Atanasoff? Atanasoff's answers to both questions was yes, and the judge was convinced by Atanasoff's testimony. Honeywell won its suit in court.

Atanasoff would have patented his own ideas about computers in the early 1940s, but he had been misled about the true design of ENIAC and had decided his own computer would find no market. Neither Atanasoff nor his co-worker Berry was ever to directly receive any money for their invention. But their years of pioneering has led to one of the most valuable machines in history. Atanasoff's crude electronic computer of the 1930s has evolved into the huge family of modern computers now in use in science, industry, the marketplace, and the home.

Almost every scientist and historian are in agreement today about the essential role of Atanasoff. He is the forgotten father of the computer.

IDENTIFYING AND PUNCTUATING THE MAIN TYPES OF SENTENCES

10

Compound Sentences

A **compound sentence,** a very common sentence pattern, contains *at least two subjects and two verbs,* usually arranged in an S-V/S-V pattern. For example:

Congress passed the bill, but the President vetoed it.
The television program received low ratings, so the network cancelled it.

In grammar, the term **compound** means "having two or more parts." Thus, the sentence "My *brother* and his *wife* are both engineers" has a **compound subject.** "The car *ran* out of gas and *stalled* in the intersection" has a **compound verb.**

A compound sentence can be divided into two parts, each of which can be a separate sentence by itself.

Congress passed the bill.
+
The President vetoed it.

The television program received low ratings.

+

The network cancelled it.

Since a compound sentence can be divided into *two* separate sentences, each half of a compound sentence must contain at least one subject and one verb. Therefore, each half of a compound sentence is a **clause.** A clause is a group of words that contains both a subject and a verb. (In contrast, a group of words that does not contain both a subject and a verb is called a **phrase,** as in a prepositional phrase.) A clause that can stand alone as a complete sentence is called an **independent clause.** Since each clause in a compound sentence can stand alone as a complete sentence, each clause must be independent. In other words:

A compound sentence consists of at least two independent clauses joined together to form a single sentence.

There are two ways to join independent clauses in order to form a compound sentence. The most frequently used method is to put a conjunction between the clauses. A **conjunction** is a word that joins words or groups of words. In grammar, the word *coordinate* means "of equal importance." Therefore, the conjunctions that are used in compound sentences are called **coordinating conjunctions** because they join two groups of words that are of equal grammatical importance. (They are both independent clauses.) The following coordinating conjunctions are used to join the clauses of compound sentences:

and
but
for (when it means *because*)
nor
or
so
yet

You should *memorize* these coordinating conjunctions because later you will have to be able to distinguish between them and the connecting words that are used to form other kinds of sentences.

In the following sentences, underline the subjects of the compound sentences *once* and the verbs *twice*, and circle the coordinating conjunction that joins the clauses. Notice that a comma **precedes** the coordinating conjunction.

The critics disliked the movie, but the public loved it.

The jury found the defendant guilty, and the judge sentenced him to five years in prison.

You can't park in this space, for it is reserved for the handicapped.

I never smoke, nor does my husband. (Notice that when *nor* is used to join two independent clauses, the pattern becomes S-V/V-S: *He has* no children, nor *has she.*)

You should move your car, or you may get a ticket.

The college needed more money, so it raised its tuition fee.

I have a good driving record, yet my car insurance costs went up.

Construct compound sentences of your own, using the coordinating conjunctions listed below to join your clauses. Underline the subject of each clause *once* and the verb *twice*. (You may construct a clause that has more than one subject and/or more than one verb, but each clause must have *at least* one subject and one verb.)

_____ , and _____

_____ , but _____

_____ , for _____

_____ , or _____

The second way to join the clauses in a compound sentence is to use a semicolon (;) *in place of both the comma and the coordinating conjunction.* For example:

I appreciate your suggestions; they have really helped me.
The test is tomorrow; we should study tonight.

Compound sentences constructed with semicolons occur less frequently than compound sentences constructed with coordinating conjunctions because some type of connecting word is usually needed to show the relationship between the clauses. For example, without a coordinating conjunction the logical relationship between the two clauses in the following sentence might be confusing.

Democracy requires a lot of patience; it is the fairest system.

If, however, you replace the semicolon with a coordinating conjunction, the relationship between the clauses becomes clear.

Democracy requires a lot of patience, *but* it is the fairest system.

It is all right to use the semicolon by itself between the clauses of a compound sentence, but do so only when the relationship between the clauses is clear without a connecting word.

Construct two compound sentences of your own, using semicolons to join the clauses. Underline the subjects *once* and the verbs *twice*. Make certain that each clause has at least one subject and one verb.

_____ ; _____

_____ ; _____

Another common way to show the relationship between the clauses of a compound sentence is to use a **conjunctive adverb,** like *however,* in the second clause. Notice that a semicolon is required between the clauses.

Democracy requires a lot of patience; *however,* it is the fairest system.

Conjunctive adverbs are especially frequent in formal language where the precise relationship between ideas is the goal. Here are most frequently used conjunctive adverbs:

also	incidentally	nonetheless
anyway	indeed	otherwise
besides	instead	still
consequently	likewise	then
finally	meanwhile	therefore
furthermore	moreover	thus
hence	nevertheless	
however	next	

A conjunctive adverb gets its double name from the fact that it does two things at once: it connects, like other **conjunctions,** and it modifies, like other **adverbs.** Because it is adverbial, it can be located in many places in its own clause. And because it can move around in the second clause and does not always come *exactly between* the two clauses (like coordinating conjunctions), it does not necessarily act as a signal to readers that they are coming to the second half of a compound sentence. For these reasons, the strong signal of a semicolon marks the end of the first clause.

> Lou wanted a challenging career; *therefore,* he became a brain surgeon.
> Lou wanted a challenging career; he, *therefore,* became a brain surgeon.
> Lou wanted a challenging career; he became a brain surgeon, *therefore.*
> Maya is a good friend; we don't, *however,* always get along.

(Notice that the conjunctive adverb is always "set off" with a comma, or two commas, in its own clause.) Construct three compound sentences of your own that use *conjunctive adverbs.* Try putting the conjunctive adverb in several different places in the second clause.

1. _____

_____

2. _____

_____

3. _____

_____

(Did you remember to "set off" the conjunctive adverb with one or two commas?)

As you can see from the sentences that you have constructed in this lesson, the following punctuation rules apply to compound sentences:

1. If the clauses in a compound sentence are joined by a coordinating conjunction, place a comma before (to the left of) the conjunction.

This sentence is compound, and it contains a comma.

You may have learned that it is not necessary to use commas in short compound sentences (for example, ''He's a Scorpio and I'm a Libra''). Although this is true, not everyone agrees on how short a ''short'' compound sentence is, so if you are in doubt, it is safer to use a comma. All the sentences in the exercises for this unit will be ''long'' compound sentences and should have a comma before the conjunction.

2. Although a compound sentence may contain more than one coordinating conjunction, the comma is placed before the conjunction that joins the clauses.

Alice *and* Ray are married, *and* they are also best friends.

3. If the clauses in a compound sentence are *not* joined by a coordinating conjunction, place a semicolon between the clauses.

Chemistry is my major; I try my hardest to make *A*'s in it.
John knew the law; however, he did not always obey it.
The candidate covered up his record; he, consequently, was able to fool the voters.

The following sentence patterns do *not* require commas because they are **simple** (meaning that they contain only one clause) rather than compound.

S-V-V   I went to the bank and deposited my check.
           (no comma)
S-S-V   Physics and chemistry are required for a
           nursing major. (no comma)
S-S-V-V   The workers and the factory owners agreed to a
           contract and prevented a strike. (no comma)

To review, the two patterns for punctuating a compound sentence are:

clause + comma + coordinating conjunction + clause
The boxer was badly injured, so the referee stopped the fight.

clause + semicolon + clause
I'm not sleeping; I'm just resting my eyelids.
I'm tired; however, I cannot sleep.

EXERCISE 10A

Make each of the following independent clauses a compound sentence by adding an appropriate coordinating conjunction and a second independent clause. Try to use as many different conjunctions in this exercise as possible. Remember to place a comma before the coordinating conjunction.

1. My sister went to this school _____

_____

2. Barry and Paul are on the wrestling team _____

_____

3. That hospital has beds for 290 patients _____

_____

4. Our team has very small players _____

_____

Write compound sentences of your own, using the coordinating conjunctions listed below. Remember to place a comma before the coordinating conjunction that divides the clauses, and make certain that each of your clauses contains at least one subject and one verb.

5. but: _____

_____

6. so: _____

_____

7. and: _____

_____

8. or: _____

_____

9. nor: _____

_____

10. for: _____

_____

11. yet: _____

_____

Construct four compound sentences punctuated with semicolons. In two of them use a conjunctive adverb in the second clause.

12. _____

_____

13. _____

_____

14. _____

_____

15. _____

_____

EXERCISE 10B

Add commas and semicolons to the following sentences wherever they are needed. If a sentence needs no additional punctuation (in other words, if the sentence is simple rather than compound), label it *C* for *correct*.

1. In the fall of 1988, three gray whales became trapped in the ice on the Alaskan coast.

2. Each fall large groups of these air-breathing mammals migrate from Alaskan waters to their breeding grounds in the tropics but somehow these three whales had failed to reach the open sea.

3. The whales were much too heavy to lift and carry to the ocean so a breathing hole in the ice was cut for them.

4. The local Eskimos began to cut a series of 8′ × 25′ holes in a path toward the ocean but the whales would not leave their original breathing hole.

5. The rescue team decided to call on the services of Jim Nollman from Friday Harbor, Washington for Nollman had the reputation of ''communicating'' with whales.

6. Nollman had already successfully attracted whales and other species by broadcasting whale calls and music through underwater hydrophones.

7. Nollman dropped his hydrophones in one of the 8′ × 25′ holes to lure the whales toward the open sea.

8. He played recorded sounds of gray whales however the whales stayed at their original hole.

9. Then he tried live guitar music still the whales would not move.

10. Next he used some recorded sounds of the three whales themselves but the whales would not leave.

11. Nollman switched to the music of *Ladysmith Black Mombazo* this rhythm group had played with Paul Simon on his hit *Graceland* album.

12. This very gentle, non-threatening music did not work either soon the Eskimos' path of breathing holes would freeze up.

13. Nollman had a new idea he dropped his hydrophone into the whales' *original* hole and played the *Black Mombazo* music.

14. Within ten seconds the whales moved to one of the Eskimos' recently-cut holes.

15. Soon the whales came back in the wrong direction but Nollman played the *Black Mombazo* music one more time.

16. This time the whales left their original hole and never turned back.

17. Eventually two of the whales, with the help of Russian icebreakers, made the three-mile trip to the freedom of the open sea.

EXERCISE 10C

All the sentence patterns listed below have multiple subjects, multiple verbs, or both. But some patterns are for *simple* sentences, and other patterns are for *compound* sentences. Write a sentence for each pattern. If a sentence is *compound*, apply one of the two punctuation rules for compound sentences.

1. S-V-V: _____

_____

_____

2. S-V-S-V: _____

_____

_____

3. S-V-V-S-V: _____

_____

_____

4. S-S-V: _____

_____

_____

5. S-V-V-V: _____

_____

_____

6. S-V-S-S-V: _____

_____

_____

7. S-S-V-V: _____

_____

_____

8. S-S-V-S-V: _____

_____

_____

Combine each pair of *simple* sentences into one *compound* sentence. Try different methods for each sentence.

9. Jack is my friend. We have some terrible arguments.

_____

_____

10. Part of us always remains childish. This fact is hard to admit.

_____

_____

11. The future is difficult to predict. Death and taxes are certain.

_____

_____

12. According to Abraham Lincoln, the *Constitution* permitted the ownership of slaves. He set them free with a special proclamation.

_____

_____

13. Many cattlemen did not believe in having sheep and cattle on the same range. This belief started many range wars in the Old West.

_____

_____

11

Complex Sentences

There are two kinds of clauses, independent and dependent. As you have seen in Lesson 8, **independent clauses** can stand alone as complete sentences. For example:

John speaks three languages.
Astronomers have discovered a new galaxy.

A **dependent clause,** however, *cannot* stand alone as a complete sentence. Instead, it must be attached to, or *depend* upon, an *independent* clause in order to form a grammatically complete sentence and to express a complete idea. Notice that the following dependent clauses are *not* complete sentences.

If it rains tomorrow . . .
Whenever I write an essay . . .
After she won the state lottery . . .

These clauses seem incomplete because they are actually only *part* of a sentence. Using the first of the following sentences as a model, change each dependent clause into a complete sentence by adding an appropriate *independent* clause.

If it rains tomorrow, ———————— *I won't wash my car.* —————————

Whenever I write an essay ——————————————————————

———————————————————————————————————————

After she won the state lottery ——————————————————————

———————————————————————————————————————

You have now constructed two complex sentences. A **complex sentence** contains both independent and dependent clauses. (In contrast, a **compound sentence** contains only *independent* clauses.)

Every dependent clause begins with a subordinating conjunction. A **conjunction** joins words or groups of words. The conjunctions that begin dependent clauses are called **subordinating conjunctions** because the word *subordinate* means "of lesser importance." Grammatically speaking, a dependent clause is "less important" than an independent clause because it cannot stand alone as a complete sentence. In contrast, the conjunctions that you used in the previous lesson to form compound sentences are called **coordinating conjunctions** because *coordinate* means "of equal importance." Since both of the clauses in a compound sentence are independent, both clauses are "of equal importance."

The type of dependent clause that you will be studying in this lesson is called an **adverb clause** because, like another adverb, an adverb clause describes a verb (or sometimes an adjective or an adverb). It is the same kind of clause that you worked with in Lesson 2. The subordinating conjunctions used to begin adverb clauses describe verbs by telling *how, when, where, why* or *under what conditions* the action occurs.

> *how:* as if, as though
> *when:* after, as, as soon as, before, until, when, whenever, while
> *where:* where, wherever
> *why:* because, in order that, since, so that
> *under what conditions:* although, as long as, even though, if, though, unless

Read the following sentences. A slanted line indicates the point at which each sentence divides into two separate clauses. Underline the subject of each clause *once* and the verb *twice*. Circle the subordinating conjunction.

Because Paul lifts weights,/he is very muscular.

When you finish the test,/you may leave.

I usually read the paper/while I eat breakfast.

Now in each sentence examine the clause that contains the circled subordinating conjunction.

The clause that contains the subordinating conjunction is the dependent clause.

Notice that in a complex sentence, the dependent clause may be either the first or the second clause in the sentence.

If you like spy stories, you should read the novels of John Le Carré.
We won't get married *until we graduate*.

In most cases, the adverb clauses in a complex sentence are *reversible*. That is, the sentence has the same basic meaning no matter which clause comes first. For example.

Whenever I buy groceries, I try to use coupons.
I try to use coupons *whenever I buy groceries*.
or

Before the game began, the crowd sang the national anthem.
The crowd sang the national anthem *before the game began*.

However, the order of the clauses in a complex sentence does affect the punctuation of the sentence.

1. If the **dependent** clause is the first clause in the sentence, it is followed by a comma.

If I have enough money, I'll buy a new car.

2. If the **independent** clause is the first clause in the sentence, no comma is needed.

I'll buy a new car *if I have enough money*.

Punctuate the following complex sentences. First circle the subordinating conjunction in each sentence, and draw a slanted line between the clauses.

I'll return your books after I eat lunch.

If you keep your old clothes long enough they'll eventually come back into fashion.

Although I can read Spanish I can't speak it well.

Unless you have a good credit rating it is difficult to borrow money from a bank.

EXERCISE 11A

Complete each of the following complex sentences by adding an appropriate adverb clause (one that makes sense in the sentence). Add commas where they are necessary.

1. When _the train left,_ we knew it was time to go.

2. Soldiers must keep in good physical condition because _they work hard._

3. Ricky ate four pieces of pie although _he does not like pie that much._

4. If _you pay me,_ I will help you study for our test.

5. As soon as _I went to work,_ the weather changed.

6. The candidate promised not to raise taxes even though _he thought they should be raised._

Construct complex sentences of your own, using the following subordinating conjunctions to form your adverb clauses. Add commas where they are necesssary.

7. _I am noticed_ wherever _I go._

8. _____I embarrassed him_____ so that
   _____his face turned red_____

9. _____I love my father_____ even though
   _____he is annoying._____

10. _____I had to leave_____ since
    _____She was ~~comi~~ going on stage_____

11. Because _I ate the pie, I had_
    allergetic reactions

Convert each pair of simple sentences below into a single complex sentence by adding a *subordinating conjunction* to the front of one of the simple sentences. Think carefully: Will either of the simple sentences make a better independent clause? Many correct combinations are possible.

12. We left early. It was raining.

    Since we left early, it was raining.

13. Lola is my sister. We rarely see each other.

    All though Lola is my sister, we rarely see each other.

14. The world will have peace. Peace is each person's deepest wish.

    Since the world will have peace, peace is each person's deepest wish.

15. Everyone uses grammar all the time. We don't think about it.

    Even though everyone uses grammer all the time, we don't think about it.

16. We campaigned vigorously for our candidate. We guaranteed her victory.

    When we campaigned vigoerously for our candidate, we guaranteed her victory

EXERCISE 11B

Determine which sentences below are *complex* by underlining their *dependent* clauses. Then add commas to the sentences if they are necessary. If a sentence needs no additional punctuation, label it *C* for *correct*.

1. All human cultures have developed time systems.

2. These systems allow humans to record past events, and to plan for the future.

3. Time systems are based on natural events like the movements of the stars and sun, because these movements occur in very regular cycles.

4. Our culture took many centuries to develop a workable calendar.

5. In our calendar, the time period of one year equals one orbit of the earth around the sun.

6. It would be convenient for us if these orbits occurred in an even number of days, like 100 days.

7. A year of exactly 100 days would have made the job of designing a calendar much easier.

8. However, the earth's orbit around the sun is not at all convenient, since it takes 365 days + 5 hours + 48 minutes + 46 seconds for the earth to circle the sun.

9. Because a year cannot be divided evenly by days, our calendar must add one day every fourth year, or *leap* year.

10. Our idea of months is based on the moon's orbit around the earth, since that occurs approximately every twenty-eight days.

11. Although each year contains twelve months, the months must be of different lengths because twelve will not go into 365 evenly.

12. In a normal year (not a leap year) we have seven months of thirty-one days, four months of thirty days, and one month of twenty-eight days, so that the twelve months will add up to 365 days for the year.

13. In leap years, the short month of February adds one day for a total of 366 days.

14. You may know the popular old rhyme to teach our calendar (the rhyme is punctuated correctly).

> Thirty days hath September,
> April, June, and November;
> February has twenty-eight alone;
> All the rest have thirty-one,
> Excepting leap year; that's the time
> When February's days are twenty-nine.

EXERCISE 11C

Part One   For each different *type* of subordinating conjunction, write a complex sentence with an adverb clause. The adverb clause may come at the beginning or at the end of the sentence.

1. a subordinating conjunction that shows *why* the action occurs:

He threw the ball, because he was angry.

2. a subordinating conjunction that shows *where* the action occurs:

If the crime was committed here, then he must have robbed them first.

3. a subordinating conjunction that shows *how* the action occurs:

4. a subordinating conjunction that shows *when* the action occurs:

5. a subordinating conjunction that shows *under what conditions* the action occurs:

Part Two Combine each pair of sentences below into a single complex sentence by joining them with a subordinating conjunction. Think carefully: Which sentence will make the best dependent clause and which conjunction will make a meaningful connection? Punctuate your new complex sentence.

6. Marshall studied hard. He took the test.

Since Marshall . . . hard, He . . .

7. Elmer started the fight. He was angry with John.

8. Her bus arrives at 11:30. We will say goodbye.

9. Harry can open this lock. We can get the door open.

12

Compound–Complex Sentences, Comma Splices, and Run-On Sentences

When a compound sentence includes a dependent clause, that type of sentence is called a **compound-complex** sentence. The dependent clause may be in either main clause.

> I will go *if you do*, but I want to stay here.
>
> or
>
> Engine-powered vehicles have replaced the horse and ox, but some people would like to go back to the "good old days" *because cars, trucks, trains, and planes make pollution and noise.*

In compound–complex sentences we can see the operation of all the punctuation rules that we have studied up to now. In the examples below of compound–complex sentences, notice how important it is to recognize the three different types of joining words: coordinating conjunctions, subordinating conjunctions, and conjunctive adverbs. (See chart inside front cover of textbook.)

The main clauses of a compound–complex sentence may be joined with a comma and a coordinating conjunction.

You should plant the garden quickly, **or** you should wait **until** the storm has blown over.

The main clauses of a compound–complex sentence may be joined with only a semicolon.

World War I was supposed to end all wars; World War II came **after** only twenty years had passed.

When a conjunctive adverb is used in the second main clause, a semicolon is needed between the main clauses.

It is very difficult to make laws about controversial issues like abortion; **however,** a law may be created **because** the public demands some resolution to the issue.

When a dependent adverbial clause comes *after* its main clause, it is *not* set off with a comma.

I like most desserts, **but** I don't eat strawberries **because** I'm allergic to them.
                                             or
I don't eat strawberries **because** I'm allergic to them, **but** I do like most desserts.

When a dependent adverbial clause comes in front of its main clause, it *is* set off with a comma.

I like most desserts, **but because** I'm allergic to strawberries, I don't eat them.
                                             or
Because I'm allergic to strawberries, I don't eat them, **but** I do like most desserts.

Run-Ons and Comma Splices

With any type of sentence, two of the most serious punctuation errors are **run-on sentences** and **comma splices.** These errors send the wrong signals to the reader, causing the reader to misread your words or confuse your meaning. (Some of the errors you corrected in the exercises for Lessons 10 and 11 were comma splices and run-ons, although they were not identified as such.)

A **run-on sentence** occurs when one sentence is run into the following sentence with no punctuation.

We respect Ann she works hard.

A **comma splice** occurs when a comma alone is used between independent clauses.

We respect Ann, she works hard.

Comma splices and run-on sentences may be corrected in several different ways. The two clauses that we looked at above may be punctuated correctly as two simple sentences.

We respect Ann. She works hard.

But you should consider other equally correct possibilities which may express a slightly different emphasis or a slightly different meaning.

We respect Ann; she works hard. (compound)
We respect Ann, for she works hard. (compound)
Ann works hard; therefore, we respect her. (compound)
We respect Ann because she works hard. (complex)

Below are some comma splices and run-ons for you to correct. Correct each one two different ways. Use a variety of punctuation and/or connecting words.

He hates computers his Mom loves them.

1. He hates computers; his Mom loves them

2. He hates computers, but his mom loves them.

121

I don't like tunnels, they scare me.

1. I don't like tunnels; they scare me.
2. I don't like tunnels because. - .

We saw a flock of geese, there were at least a dozen.

1. _____

_____

2. _____

_____

Though all sharks have common traits, they come in many different sizes and shapes each species is adapted to a particular prey and a particular hunting pattern.

1. _____

_____

_____

2. _____

_____

_____

I am enjoying my psychology class it makes me think about the reasons for my behavor.

1. _____

_____

2. _____

_____

Comma splices and run-ons usually occur in definite patterns for different writers. For example, many writers often make these errors when a clause begins with a subject pronoun referring to a noun in the previous clause (as in the final sentence you corrected above). To find out if you have a definite pattern in the way that you make these errors, keep a list of your comma splices and run-ons. After you have collected half a dozen or more, go over them with your teacher. If you can discover a pattern, you will find it easier to keep from making these punctuation errors.

EXERCISE 12A

Part One   All of the sentences below are compound–complex. Study each sentence carefully. Circle the subordinating conjunction and underline its dependent clause. (Which *independent* clause does it belong to?) Punctuate the whole sentence as a compound sentence. Then, if necessary, set off the dependent clause with a comma.

1. The weather conditions were bad, but we continued because we were late.

2. The game was over, and we felt good although we had lost.

3. Although the car is expensive, it has a poor frequency-of-repair record; its resale value is also extremely low.

4. The campaign began at a slow pace, but after the candidates debated on national television, it picked up speed and rolled into high gear.

5. Although the shooting took place in broad daylight, no one saw it, and no one reported it.

6. The company went bankrupt after its sales dropped, yet its employees continued to trust the company officers.

7. If her invention succeeds in getting a patent, she will market it herself; we will do the packaging.

8. The horse was exhausted; however, until the race was over, the rider kept spurring and whipping it.

9. Jones apologized, for he knew it was wrong as soon as he did it.

10. The plane exploded as it fell; no one survived.

11. Grace was discouraged; nevertheless, since the project had been her idea, she stuck it out to the end.

Part Two   Compose four compound-complex sentences and punctuate them carefully.

12. You could go to school quickly, or you could wait until the rain stops.

13. This essay was supposed to be the end of essays; another essay was assigned after only 2 years.

14. I like a lot of pizzas, but because pizza is so fattening, I don't eat it that often.

15. It is very difficult to make stories about unusual topics; however, stories are rewarding after they are written.

EXERCISE 12B

The essay below includes simple, compound, complex, and compound–complex sentences, but they are not always punctuated correctly. Some of the errors are comma splices and run-on sentences; other errors are less serious. Correct all the errors.

Since I was a small boy, I have loved to play football; in junior high and high school I played for my school teams. I became first-string quarterback in my sophomore year of high school, and in my junior year our team won the state championship. We expected to repeat the championship in my senior year, but that did not happen.

It was nice to be a football star in high school; most of the students looked up to me, and I never lacked for dates with all of the prettiest girls. This was a good life for a person from a family on welfare. Because my family was so poor, my dream was to star in college football too, and then to become a highly-paid professional player. After we became state champs, the sportwriters called me, "The Million-Dollar Arm," that was not much of an exaggeration because the college coaches began to recruit me heavily.

Many recruiters from all over the country came to our dilapidated, old house to get me to commit myself to their colleges. When I told them I couldn't make up my mind, they would just offer me bigger scholarships and more benefits. I understood the meaning of the "benefits": they would probably include a free car, an apartment, and an easy job for high pay. I was ready for all those nice things, but Fate had other plans for my future.

In November of my senior year, we played our Homecoming Game on the day after Thanksgiving. We were ahead 19–6 in the second quarter. Just after I threw a pass, I was hit low from the side, and my knee snapped. I passed out from the pain and woke up in the hospital. I have not played football since that night. I walk with a slight limp, and my knee still hurts a lot even though I have had two operations. Now I'm just an ordinary student in a community college.

I have yet to accept the idea of *not* being a rich, famous athlete. That dream is dying hard.

EXERCISE 12C

Below are several groups of simple sentences. Combine each group into a single compound–complex sentence by using the various ways for connecting clauses that we've studied in the past three lessons. Word your new sentence so that it makes sense and reads smoothly. (Several combinations are possible. You might want to try each sentence first on a piece of scratch paper.) The first sentence combination has been done as an example.

1. Rex did not pass the qualifying test for deep-sea diving.
   He will not become a certified diver.
   He is very disappointed.

   Because Rex did not pass the qualifying test for deep-sea diving, he will not become a certified diver; he is very disappointed.

2. Irene is very strong.
   She is too slow for basketball.
   She is going to try out for weightlifting.

   Although Irene is very strong, she is too slow for basketball, but she will try out for weightlifting

3. World peace depends on the powerful nations.
   The can save the world.
   They can destroy the world.

   _____

   _____

   _____

4. Good health care may prolong one's life.
Not everyone can afford good health care.
It isn't cheap.

_____

_____

_____

5. Each generation invents its own slang.
Some slang words become respectable and become a permanent part of
the language.
The slang origin of such words is often forgotten.

_____

_____

_____

6. Marxist societies have emphasized economic equality.
Democratic societies have emphasized political equality.
These kinds of equality are interdependent.

_____

_____

_____

_____

7. English has only twenty-six letters.
It has forty-three sounds.
English is not an easy language to spell.

_____

_____

_____

13

Correcting Fragments

The basic unit of expression in written English is the sentence. As you already know, *a sentence must contain at least one independent clause*.

If you take a group of words that is *not* a complete sentence and punctuate it as though it were a complete sentence, you have created a **sentence fragment.** In other words, you have written only a piece – a fragment – of a sentence rather than a complete sentence.

As you can see. Wrong punctuation. May be confusing.

Since semicolons and periods are usually interchangeable, fragments may also be created by misusing semicolons.

As you can see; wrong punctuation may be confusing.

If you look carefully at the two groups of words, you see that they should form a single, complex sentence which needs, at most, a comma.

As you can see, wrong punctuation may be confusing.

Although fragments occur frequently in speech and occasionally in informal writing, they are generally not acceptable in classroom writing and should be avoided in formal writing situations.

There are two types of fragments: **dependent clauses** and **phrases.**

As you have already learned (Lesson 11), a dependent clause cannot stand alone as a complete sentence. It must be attached to an independent clause in order to form a complex sentence.

Therefore, any dependent clause that is separated from its main clause by a period or semicolon is a fragment.

Below are several examples of this type of fragment.

When we exercise vigorously. We inhale more oxygen.
When we exercise vigorously; we inhale more oxygen.
We inhale more oxygen. When we exercise vigorously.
We inhale more oxygen; when we exercise vigorously.

Eliminate the dependent-clause fragments in the following paragraph by punctuating them correctly.

Textbooks for most classes may be purchased; before the class meets. However, some professors do not want their students to purchase any texts. Until the class has met for at least one session. These professors may use the first class session to check each student's eligibility for that course. If the student is not eligible; he or she will not be allowed to remain in the course, and the student won't be the owner of an unwanted textbook. Most students like this policy. Because the bookstore will not refund the full purchase price. When an unused book is returned.

Are you remembering to punctuate each dependent clause according to its location? As you learned in Lesson 11, if the *dependent* clause is the first clause in a sentence, it should be followed by a comma. If the *independent* clause is the first clause in a sentence, no comma is needed.

The second type of fragment is the phrase. Since a **phrase** is defined as a group of words that does *not* contain both a subject and a verb, a phrase obviously cannot be a complete sentence. **All phrases are fragments.** Study the following types of fragments, and notice the way each phrase has been changed from a fragment into a complete sentence.

FRAGMENT – NO SUBJECT	Didn't finish the book.
SENTENCE	*John* didn't finish the book.
FRAGMENT – NO VERB	The cheerleaders on the field.
SENTENCE	The cheerleaders *are* on the field.
FRAGMENT – INCOMPLETE VERB (*-ing* form)	The cat watching the dog.
SENTENCE	The cat *was watching* the dog.
	(An *-ing* main verb must be preceded by a helping verb)
	or
	The cat watch*es* the dog.
	(Change the *-ing* form of the verb)
FRAGMENT – INCOMPLETE VERB (past participle)	The picture painted by Diana.
SENTENCE	The picture *was painted* by Diana.
	(To be a main verb, a past participle must be preceded by a helping verb. For an explanation and a list of past participles, see Lesson 26.)
FRAGMENT – INFINITIVE	To do the assignment correctly.
SENTENCE	*He wants* to do the assignment correctly.
FRAGMENT – PARTICIPLE	Watching Maria smile.
SENTENCE	*I like* watching Maria smile.

The following groups of words are fragments because they lack either a subject or a verb or because they have an incomplete verb. Rewrite each fragment so that it becomes a complete sentence.

To eliminate the funny noise in the motor.

Returning your phone call.

The film damaged by exposure to light.

Mailed your package for you.

The most expensive item on the menu.

The lineman accidentally tackled by the safety.

The candidates appearing in a debate.

When you are writing a composition, be careful not to separate a phrase from the rest of the sentence to which it belongs.

INCORRECT   I've lost a small boy. Wearing red pants.
  CORRECT   I've lost a small boy wearing red pants.
INCORRECT   Smiling from her victory; she took the prize.
  CORRECT   Smiling from her victory, she took the prize.

Rewrite the following items so that any fragmentary phrases are correctly joined with the sentences to which they belong.

The voters were angry. They signed a petition. Asking for a reduction in

property taxes.

My appointment was for late afternoon. Hoping to avoid heavy traffic; I

left my office at 3:00.

Lulled by the motion of the car. The child fell asleep in her car-seat.

To summarize: **phrases** are sentence fragments because they do not contain both a subject and a complete verb. (In other words, they are not clauses.) **Dependent clauses** are fragments because they are not *independent* clauses. This is simply another way of stating the most basic rule of sentence construction:

Every sentence must contain at least one independent clause.

EXERCISE 13A

In the essay below, some phrases and dependent clauses have been separated by periods or semicolons from the independent clauses to which they belong. Locate these *fragments* and correct them by attaching each to the correct independent clause. In some cases you should replace the period or semicolon with a comma, but in other cases no punctuation is required. You may need to change some capital letters to lower case letters.

1. A nationwide effort made by blacks and their supporters in the 1950s and 1960s. The "civil rights movement" was a largely successful attempt to end segregation and gain equal civil rights for minorities. The first widely publicized event in the movement was a bus boycott in Montgomery, Alabama. Sparked by the refusal of one black woman, Rosa Parks, to surrender her bus seat to a white person. The boycott was non-violent but effective. Because the bus system began to lose money. The boycott was followed by a number of sit-ins and demonstrations. Widely seen by millions on national television.

2. Gathering by the hundreds of thousands; civil rights marchers converged on Washington, D.C., in 1963. At this giant rally in the nation's capital. Martin Luther King, Jr., made his famous "I Have a Dream" speech. With reporters and cameras present from the

entire world. The political leaders of the nation could not ignore the pressure for change. Authorizing federal action against segregation in public accommodations, public facilities, and employment; the Civil Rights Act of 1964 passed Congress and was signed into law.

3. Met by violent police responses. Civil rights demonstrators in Selma, Alabama, protested against systematic denial of the voting rights of blacks. In 1965 the Voting Rights Act was passed in the United States Congress. After another three years of pressure from the movement. The Fair Housing Act was passed in 1968.

4. With many of its legislative goals accomplished; the civil rights movement now turned its attention. In the direction of education and of changing the attitudes of whites. For some blacks the movement did not move far enough or fast enough. They formed much more militant groups. Only a few of these groups continued after the 1970s.

5. Not all of the civil rights legislation has survived tests in court. Denied admission to a California medical school that had admitted black candidates with weaker academic credentials. Allan Bakke, a white man, fought his case all the way to the Supreme Court. Contending that he was the victim of racial discrimination. The Court ruled in Bakke's favor. In the same case, however, the Court ruled

that medical schools were entitled to consider race as one factor in admissions. Thus upholding the important civil rights principle of affirmative action.

6. Though the civil rights movement did not reach all its goals, it has achieved much of what it set out to do. Accomplishing many changes through such non-violent means as voter registration, carefully planned marches and demonstrations, and civil disobedience. Today we see other movements such as the "right-to-life" movement and the "Farm-Aid" movement; using the tactics that worked for civil rights.

EXERCISE 13B

Each of the paragraphs below contains *comma splices, run-on sentences,* and *fragments.* Correct these errors using the methods you have learned from this lesson and the previous lesson.

1. The appendix is a small, closed tube projecting from the large intestine on the right side of the body. Although everyone has an appendix, No one has been able to discover its purpose. Medical scientists believe it is a remnant from some previous structure in the digestive system. Apparently the structure became useless during the course of human evolution; most people go through life paying no attention to the appendix. But occasionally the appendix may become the site of severe and life-threatening infection. This may happen When waste matter accumulates and hardens in the appendix. The resulting appendicitis causes severe pain in the abdomen, fever, nausea, vomiting and muscle spasms. Appendicitis may occur at any age Although it is most common for people under twenty. If a victim is wrongly given laxatives or an enema, The appendix may rupture, Causing the even more serious disorder of

peritonitis. When appendicitis is detected in time, it is treated with surgery and antibiotics the chances of complete recovery are excellent.

2. A basic principle of American government is the "separation of powers." Under this principle the powers of government are divided among three distinct branches called the executive branch, the legislative branch, and the judicial branch. Officials for each branch are selected by different procedures and serve for different terms of office, through a system of "checks and balances" set forth in the Constitution any one branch may block the actions of another branch. An example of this blocking occurs when Congress votes not to give the President money to carry out some executive program. Throughout our history the separation of powers has proved the wisdom of the framers of the Constitution they did not want any one branch ever to accumulate too much power. They also wanted to guarantee the careful consideration of all important issues by the government before any action was taken.

3. Satire is a form of art. It ridicules its subject by comparing it to some ethical or moral or artistic standard. Although most satire is literary, it is also found in the graphic arts (like painting, drawing,

and photography), in sculpture, and even in music. Satire may attack

individuals like politicians or generals, It may attack such groups

As political parties, religious denominations, or car manufacturers.

It may also attack policies or ideas. Like the policy of "the cold war"

or the idea of "all men are equal." Repressive societies are uncom-

fortable with satire, Because it may be turned against them. Satire

flourishes in open societies, Even though that very openness may

be satirized.

EXERCISE 13C

Show that you understand what a *comma splice* is by writing three of them.
After you write each comma splice, correct it in the space provided. Use a different method to correct each one.

1. _She hates horses, I love them._

   correction: _She hates horses; I love them._

2. _I think she is pretty, you are not._

   correction: _I think she is pretty, but you are not._

3. _She got kicked in soccer, was not hurt._

   correction: _She got kicked in soccor; although, she was not hurt._

Show that you understand what a *run-on sentence* is by writing three of them.
After you write each run-on, correct it in the space provided. Use a different
method to correct each one.

1. _Although I love basketball I suck at it._

   correction: _Although I love basketball, I suck at it._

2. Although Steph believes school is getting harder it is not.

correction: Although Steph believes school is getting harder, it is not.

3. I got kicked out of the library I was eating.

correction: I got kicked out of the library; I was eating

Show that you understand what *fragments* are by writing three different kinds of fragments. After you write each fragment, correct it in the space provided.

1. Because I love him.

correction: He is nice because I love him,

2. Causing him to be mad.

correction: Ayla was insolent, causing him to be mad.

3. To stop her from running.

correction: He held her to stop her from running.

Correcting Comma Splices, Run-On
Sentences and Fragments
Unit Review

Correct any comma splices, run-on sentences, or fragments in the following paragraphs.

1. Bank robbers today sometimes take an innocent hostage so that the police will leave them alone. While they make their escape from the bank. Terrorists take hostages to force their demands on others. They may demand money, or a safe passage from a hijacking, or the release of their jailed comrades. The use of hostages to force others to do as you wish is not a new custom, it is a very old one.

2. When an ancient king conquered new territory, he could try to assure himself of future peace by slaughtering all the males of fighting age, however this slaughter might ruin the economy of his newly conquered country a more practical and humane way to pacify the territory was to take hostages, the conquering king would take as prisoners to his own country a carefully selected group like the wives and children of all the important people. As long as the conquered territory behaved itself; the group of hostages would live in safety and good health. If the people in the conquered territory did not remain peaceful, they knew their loved ones would die.

3. In the Middle Ages a very strict code concerning hostages

developed. During the Hundred Years War, a group of French hostages was sent to England in exchange for the release of King John II of France. When the hostages later escaped; King John felt bound by his honor to return to captivity in England.

4. Until the 18th century civilian or military hostages were often exchanged. After treaties were concluded. To guarantee the fulfillment of the treaty. In the 19th and early 20th centuries, the practice of using hostages came under increasing criticism. Especially the taking of civilian hostages. The most recent large-scale use of civilian hostages occurred in World War II. In countries under German occupation, the authorities took thousands of civilian hostages throughout Europe. In an attempt to suppress resistance movements against the German armies. These authorities finally executed huge numbers of these hostages. Because the resistance movements continued to resist the occupation of their homelands. After World War II was over; most of the countries in the world signed an addition to the Geneva Convention, they agreed to stop entirely from taking civilian hostages anywhere in the world.

5. As we know from the daily news. This prohibition is widely ignored. By various rebel groups throughout the world. And by many established governments.

PUNCTUATION THAT "SETS OFF" OR SEPARATES

14

Parenthetical Expressions

When speaking, people often interrupt their sentences with expressions such as *by the way, after all,* or *as a matter of fact.* These expressions are not really part of the main idea of the sentence; instead, they are interrupting — or **parenthetical** — expressions which speakers use to fill in the pauses while they are thinking of what to say next. In speech, people indicate that these parenthetical expressions are not part of the main idea of the sentence by pausing and dropping their voices before and after the expression. In writing, the same pauses are indicated with commas.

You have already learned that commas may be used to separate the clauses in compound and complex sentences. Another major function of the comma is to "set off" interrupting, or **parenthetical expressions** from the rest of the sentence in which they occur.

Read the following sentences aloud, and notice how the commas around the italicized parenthetical expressions correspond to the pauses you make in speech.

Well, the bus is late again.
This morning, *in fact,* it is almost twenty minutes late.
I'm going to be late for work, *I'm afraid.*

The rule for punctuating parenthetical expressions is very simple:

A parenthetical expression must be completely set off from the rest of the sentence by commas.

This means that if the parenthetical expression occurs at the *beginning* of the sentence, it is *followed* by a comma. For example:

On the whole, married men live longer than single men.

If the parenthetical expression is at the *end* of the sentence, it is *preceded* by a comma.

The capital of Michigan is Lansing, isn't it?

If the parenthetical expression is in the *middle* of the sentence, it is both *preceded* and *followed* by a comma.

Coal and diamonds, for example, both contain carbon.

There are many parenthetical expressions. Some of the most frequently used ones are listed below.

after all
as a matter of fact
at any rate
etc. (an abbreviation of the Latin words *et cetera*, meaning "and other things")
for example
for instance
furthermore
however
in fact
nevertheless
of course
on the other hand
on the whole
therefore
well (at the beginning of a sentence)
yes and *no* (at the beginning of a sentence)

Expressions such as the following are often parenthetical if they occur in a position *other than* at the beginning of a sentence.

does it
doesn't it
I believe
I suppose
I hope
I think
is it
isn't it
that is
you know

For example:

Today is payday, isn't it?
Eggs, you know, are high in cholesterol.

Continual repetition of the parenthetical expression *you know* should be avoided in both speech and writing. If you are speaking clearly and your listener is paying attention, he knows what you are saying and does not have to be constantly reminded of the fact. Besides, you know, continually repeating *you know* can be irritating to your listener; and, you know, it doesn't really accomplish anything.

Study the following points carefully.

1. Some of the above words and phrases can be either parenthetical or not parenthetical, depending upon how they are used in a sentence. **If an expression is parenthetical, it can be removed from the sentence, and the remaining words will still be a complete sentence.**

PARENTHETICAL	Congress, *after all*, represents the people.
NOT PARENTHETICAL	She was tired *after all* her work.
PARENTHETICAL	Ms. Walker's prose is better than her poetry, *I think*.
NOT PARENTHETICAL	Often *I think* about my childhood friends.

2. Since the abbreviation *etc.* is parenthetical, it must be *preceded* and *followed* by a comma if it occurs in the middle of a sentence.

Shirts, ties, shaving lotion, *etc.*, are typical Father's Day gifts.

The final comma after *etc.* indicates that *etc.* is parenthetical. Notice that this comma serves a different function from the commas that separate the items in the series.

3. **Conjunctive adverbs,** like *however* and *nevertheless*, are considered parenthetical and are set off in the clause in which they occur. They should be punctuated in simple sentences as follows:

I don't like him. *However,* he is a good man to work for.

or

I don't like him. He is, *however,* a good man to work for.

In the second clause of a compound sentence, **conjunctive adverbs** should be punctuated as follows:

He is a good friend; *however,* we often disagree.
She didn't study much; *nevertheless,* she received a *B*.

(Conjunctive adverbs have been discussed earlier in Unit Four. For a complete list of them see the inside front cover.)

4. People's names and titles are also set off by commas **if you are speaking directly to them** in a sentence. This type of construction is called **direct address.** The punctuation of direct address is the same as that used for parenthetical expressions.

Ladies and gentlemen of the jury, have you reached a verdict?
Mrs. Castro, will you speak to our club?

Notice that names and titles are set off by commas only when the person is being *directly addressed* in the sentence. Otherwise, no commas are needed.

The package is for Donald. (no comma)
Donald, did you get the package? (comma for direct address)

EXERCISE 14A

Part One Add commas to the following sentences wherever they are necessary. If a sentence needs no additional punctuation, label it *C* for *correct*. The sentences in this section of the exercise deal only with the punctuation of parenthetical expressions.

1. Speaking a language is easier than writing it isn't it?

2. After all we've been speaking since we were small children.

3. We learn to speak in fact without school or homework.

4. We can speak without knowing how to spell can't we?

5. There are however some very big advantages to writing.

Part Two Add commas and semicolons to the following sentences wherever they are necessary. If a sentence needs no additional punctuation, label it *C* for *correct*. This section covers the punctuation of compound and complex sentences as well as parenthetical expressions and direct address.

6. Although writing takes longer, it usually makes us think more carefully about what we're saying doesn't it?

7. It's true I know that speakers get immediate feedback from their listeners; on the other hand writers know that readers may take more time and may even re-read to make sure they understand.

8. Furthermore writing is usually a much more permanent form of expression because it's usually easier to save the written word.

9. Written language changes very slowly over the centuries consequently we can today read and understand writings like our two-hundred-year-old *Constitution.*

10. However because the pronunciation of spoken language changes with each new generation of speakers it might be quite difficult to understand the speech of Shakespeare or indeed George Washington.

11. Even today the regional differences of dialects in English like our Southern speech in the United States or the speech of Australians like Crocodile Dundee sometimes make it very difficult for visiting speakers of English to converse in the local dialect.

12. No *reader* of English however would have trouble reading and understanding today's newspaper in Alabama or in Sydney, Australia.

13. Yes reader speaking is "easier" than writing but writing is nonetheless indispensable for certain purposes.

EXERCISE 14B

Add commas and semicolons to the following sentences wherever they are necessary. If a sentence needs no additional punctuation, label it *C* for *correct.* This exercise covers the punctuation of compound and complex sentences and parenthetical expressions.

1. One in every hundred people is affected with the mental disorder of schizophrenia.

2. Its symptoms include difficulty in thinking and concentrating, erratic behavior, very inappropriate emotional responses, hallucinations, and delusions consequently schizophrenia is considered one of the most serious mental illnesses.

3. Many doctors have blamed schizophrenia on the home environment because some patients clearly improved after they were taken out of their homes.

4. On the other hand some researchers have looked for the cause of this disorder in the patient's heredity since schizophrenia did seem to run in families.

5. One percent of the total population has schizophrenia however the rate is 10 percent among close family members of a schizophrenic and the rate is 50 percent among identical twins if one is already a victim.

6. Moreover whenever the children of schizophrenic mothers are placed for adoption shortly after birth 16 percent of them develop the disorder.

7. Statistics like these from the past thirty years suggest an extremely close link between schizophrenia and heredity but until recently researchers had no concrete evidence for such a link.

8. A new report in the journal *Nature* may offer the first solid clue about the cause or causes of schizophrenia.

9. A team of British and American scientists studied the genetic material from seven selected families among the 104 members of the these families were thirty-nine schizophrenics.

10. The genetic material indicated that all thirty-nine of the disordered family members shared a specific piece of DNA containing an abnormal gene, or hereditary unit.

11. Not every schizophrenic seems to share this abnormal gene nevertheless this study points to a genetic abnormality of some type as the cause of all schizophrenia.

12. Our new understanding about the origin of this very tragic disease should have some clear benefits.

13. We may for example soon be able to identify people likely to develop the disease and monitor them for the earliest possible treatment.

14. Eventually researchers may design tests for prenatal screening of some forms of schizophrenia.

15. Scientists hope of course we will someday learn how to ''repair'' most genetic abnormalities so that diseases like schizophrenia will be found only in the history books.

EXERCISE 14C

Add commas and semicolons to the following letter wherever they are necessary. This exercise covers the punctuation of compound and complex sentences and parenthetical expressions.

Dear Mrs. Johnson,

I thought about speaking to you in person but after I gave the matter some more thought it seemed best to write you a letter. Sometimes parents are I know just too busy or preoccupied to see when their children are straying from the right path.

A few nights ago when you and your husband were away from home I noticed a light on in your bedroom. I think it's your bedroom because the shade is always down.

Well on this night the shades were up and I'm sure you wouldn't approve of the goings-on in your bedroom. Your daughter Irene was trying on all of your clothes Mrs. Johnson! She even put on items like your red mini skirt. It's the very tight one you know. I don't think you've worn it for over a year. I didn't say anything to you because I know that teenagers are full of life and don't always think about the consequences of their actions. In fact I didn't even get too upset when she saw me through the window, shouted, "Take that, you old bat!" and jerked down the shade. I was after all once a teenager myself. Besides I know it's not easy for you to raise teen-age triplets.

Last Saturday night, your daughter Luella and that giant boyfriend of hers roared into your driveway at two in the morning and sat with his car stereo going full blast until dawn consequently I got three hours of sleep that night. I could have called the police of course but I thought Luella and Greaseball must be keeping you and your husband awake too. That is until I learned that you and Mr. Johnson were out of town and therefore must have gotten a sound night's sleep.

I've really been very patient with your girls' wild ways I think. However yesterday afternoon was the straw that broke the camel's back. I always considered your daughter Alma to be the sweetest of your three girls. Well I guess she's sweet all right. When I heard a lot of giggling outside I peeked through the window. There was your Alma sitting on your patio in broad daylight. Was she with a boy? No she was sitting with a boy *on each side of her* and they were kissing her right and left. I don't know how the poor girl could breathe!

I could have broken it up but I thought I'd better just watch for a while in case Alma needed any help.

Mrs. Johnson you are just going to have to make those girls behave. Because I was so tired today from worrying about Irene and Luella and keeping an eye on Alma I missed every one of my soaps on the television.

Your concerned neighbor,
Iva Birdseye

15

Appositives

In sentences you sometimes use a noun whose meaning may not be as clear to your reader as it is to you. For example, suppose that you write:

Estivation is used by some desert animals to survive summer's heat.

If you think that your reader may not know what estivation is, you can add a phrase to your sentence to provide more information about estivation.

Estivation, *a slowing down of the body's processes,* is used by some desert animals to survive summer's heat.

This kind of explanatory phrase is called an **appositive** (from the verb *to appose,* meaning "to place things beside each other"). An appositive is a phrase placed beside a noun in order to clarify that noun's meaning. Study the following sentences, in which the appositives have been italicized. Notice that each appositive *immediately follows the noun it describes.*

John Bilson, *the senior senator in Congress,* will be the speaker.
Thursday is named for Thor, *a god of Scandinavian mythology.*

The city of Williamsburg, *the center of Virginia's colonial government,* is now a great tourist attraction.

As you can see, appositives must be set off by commas from the rest of the sentence just as parenthetical expressions are. Appositives are considered *extra* elements in a sentence because they add additional information about a noun that has already been *specifically identified*. For example, in the first sentence above, even without the appositive "the senior senator in Congress," you know which person will be the speaker because he has already been specifically identified as *John Bilson*. In the second sentence, even without the appositive "a god of Scandinavian mythology," the person after whom Thursday is named has already been specifically identified as *Thor*. Similarly, in the third sentence, even without the appositive "a center of Virginia's colonial government," you know that the city which is a great tourist attraction is specifically *Williamsburg*.

Here is the rule for punctuating this kind of explanatory phrase or clause:

If a phrase or clause adds additional information about a noun that has already been specifically identified, that phrase or clause must be completely set off from the rest of the sentence by commas.

In this lesson, you will be dealing with appositives, which are phrases. In Lesson 16, you will be applying the same rule to clauses.

Specifically identified includes mentioning either a person's first or last name, or both, or using words such as "my oldest brother," "my ten o'clock class on Monday," or "my hometown." The nouns in these last three phrases are considered to be *specifically identified* because even though you have not mentioned your brother's name, you can have only one "oldest" brother. Similarly, only one specific town can be your "hometown." In other words, *specifically identified* means limiting the meaning of a general word like *town* to *one particular* town or limiting a general word like *class* to *one particular* class.

Underline the appositives in the following sentences, and then punctuate them. Remember that appositives *follow* the nouns that they describe.

I will leave next Monday the day after my birthday.

English everyone's favorite subject is a required course.

Have you been to our nation's capital Washington, D.C.?

My cousin Pam the only girl in her family wants to coach football.

The plane in the movie was a DC-3 a favorite of many old pilots.

World View a series of tours of ancient civilizations will begin its first tour

in March.

On the other hand, if a phrase is *necessary* to establish the specific identity of a noun, it is *not* set off by commas. Study the difference between the following pair of sentences.

The novel *Great Expectations* is considered by many critics to be Charles Dickens' greatest work. (No commas are used to set off *Great Expectations* because the title is necessary to identify which of Dickens' many novels is considered to be his greatest work.)
Charles Dickens' fourteenth novel, *Great Expectations*, is considered by many critics to be his greatest work. (Commas are used to set off *Great Expectations* because Dickens' greatest work has already been specifically identified as his *fourteenth novel.*)

Most single-word appositives are necessary to establish the specific identity of the nouns they follow and are, therefore, *not* set off by commas.

My sister *Elizabeth* is married to Tim Nolan.
The word *microfiche* means "a sheet of microfilm."
Certain tones of the color *red* are known to increase anxiety.

Underline the appositives in the following sentences, and then add commas wherever they are necessary. Some sentences may not require commas.

Ben Johnson one of the greatest runners in history tarnished his reputation

by using steroids in the 1988 Olympics.

Pitcairn's Island a small dot in the southeastern Pacific Ocean was settled

by a boatload of British mutineers.

My friend Lila has over twenty different books about jewelry.

Kudzu grass a non-native plant in the United States has invaded many areas

of the South and costs millions of dollars to control.

The word *mercurial* comes from the personal traits of the Greek God Mercury.

Pennsylvania is named after William Penn a leader of colonial America.

EXERCISE 15A

Add commas to the following sentences wherever they are necessary.

1. The plantain a variety of banana is cooked as a main dish in many parts of the world.

2. Her daughter captain of two varsity teams won a college scholarship for her athletic ability.

3. The toyon bush *heteromeles acutifolia* beautifies much of the coastal landscape of the Pacific states.

4. I sent the package to my cousin Lavelle.

5. Algebra the most difficult course on my schedule has a good teacher.

6. The costly film *Gone with the Wind* paid for itself quickly.

7. Our coach had the bad habit of misspelling the word *dumb*.

8. Midway an island in the center of the Pacific Ocean was the setting for one of history's great naval battles.

9. My oldest sister Rosa is my best friend.

10. They watched a film about Gabon a country in West Africa.

11. The Bengals put their tallest player Williams up against the shortest player on the Beavers' team Schwarznegger.

12. Beethoven's best known symphony the *Fifth Symphony* is believed to express the composer's love for human liberty.

EXERCISE 15B

Add commas and semicolons to the following sentences wherever they are necessary. If a sentence needs no additional punctuation, label it *C* for *correct*. This exercise covers punctuation rules from previous lessons as well as the punctuation of appositives.

1. About 200 years ago a French engineer invented a most revolutionary machine.

2. That Frenchman Nicolas Joseph Cugnot built the first self-propelled vehicle in 1789 and it was soon called an "auto-mobile."

3. Cugnot's vehicle a heavy carriage with three wheels was powered by a steam engine.

4. The vehicle moved at a snail's pace three miles per hour but it proved the concept of self-propulsion.

5. Over the next forty years many inventors tried to develop better steam-powered automobiles.

6. Newly formed companies in England attempted to operate the new vehicles commercially on regular schedules however their opponents in some counties had these "noisy and frightening monsters" banned from the roads.

7. Competing businesses with their money in horse-drawn transportation did not want the new inventions to take away their jobs and incomes.

8. To retard development of self-propelling vehicles, these opponents of the automobile used excessive tolls on bridges and roads and limited the speed of the new vehicle to four miles per hour.

9. A special law the Red Flag Act required a man with a red flag to *walk* in front of each steam-powered auto.

10. A big breakthrough for self-propulsion came with the development of a better power source the internal-combustion engine.

11. The first vehicle with this source of power was probably the one tried in 1885 by a German engineer Karl Benz.

12. Gottlieb Daimler another German engineer soon built a much better internal-combustion engine the modern automobile was born.

13. The profit-making possibilities encouraged extremely rapid growth of the gas-powered vehicle this new, cheap, powerful vehicle would cause worldwide changes in our patterns of behavior and a radically-changed look to the landscape of planet Earth.

14. Steam-powered vehicles the first "auto-mobiles" continued in production until after World War I but they were eventually put out of business by the lighter, more efficient, gas-powered vehicles.

EXERCISE 15C

Part One   The sentences below are arranged in pairs. Combine each pair into a third sentence. Use information from the second sentence *to create an appositive in the first sentence.* Decide whether you should set off the appositive with commas. The first pair has been done as an example:

1. a. My brother works for the city.

 b. My brother's name is John.

 c. *My brother John works for the city.*

2. a. My mother made paella for dinner.

 b. Paella is a rich Spanish casserole.

 c. _____

3. a. Carol went to Meadville for the holidays.

 b. Meadville is Carol's hometown.

 c. _____

4. a. My co-worker is sick.

 b. My co-worker's name is Mike.

 c. _____

5. a. Mable Lee's latest novel is a best seller.

 b. The novel is titled *Sin.*

 c. _____

6. a. Nephritis attacks the kidneys.

   b. Nephritis is an auto-immune disease.

   c. _____

7. a. We spent our vacation at Lake Tahoe.

   b. Lake Tahoe is my mom's favorite place.

   c. _____

8. a. The baking soda worked very well.

   b. Baking soda is a product with many uses.

   c. _____

Part Two   Add appositive phrases to the following sentences. If necessary, set off the appositives with commas. The first two sentences have been done as examples.

9. My brother _____*John*_____ graduated in 1988.

10. The White House _*, the official residence of the President,*_ is in Washington, D.C.

11. Of all my cousins, my cousin _____ is the most like me.

12. That stereo _____ costs too much.

13. My physics teacher _____ livens up his lectures with practical jokes.

14. He gave her a ring featuring her birthstone _____.

15. The movie _____ is my favorite.

16. We showed the tourists a big attraction _____.

16

Restrictive and
Nonrestrictive Clauses

In Lesson 15 you learned that if a phrase adds extra information about a noun that has already been specifically identified, that phrase (an **appositive**) must be set off by commas. For example:

Albert Einstein, the great scientist, wrote passionate love letters.

The appositive is set off by commas because the person who wrote passionate love letters has already been specifically identified as Einstein.

On the other hand, if a phrase is *necessary* to establish the specific identity of a noun, the phrase is *not* set off by commas.

The movie *Star Wars* is based on very old legends.

The phrase *Star Wars* is not set off by commas because it is necessary to identify which specific movie is based on very old legends.

The same rule that applies to the punctuation of appositive phrases also applies to the punctuation of *clauses*. Read the following sentences, in which the dependent clauses have been italicized. Can you see why one sentence in each pair has commas while the other does not?

The man *who invented dynamite* established a famous prize for world peace. Alfred Nobel, *who invented dynamite,* established a famous prize for world peace.

A board game *which is based on the private ownership of property* is now very popular in communist China.

The board game of Monopoly, *which is based on the private ownership of property,* is now very popular in communist China.

In the first sentence of each pair, the dependent clause is necessary to establish the specific identity of the noun it follows. This type of clause is called a **restrictive clause** because it *restricts,* or limits, the meaning of the word it describes. For example, in the first sentence if the restrictive clause were removed, the sentence would read:

The man established a famous prize for world peace.

The meaning of this sentence is unclear since there are millions of men in the world, and any one of them might have established a peace prize. But when the clause is added to the sentence, the meaning of the general word *man* is now *restricted,* or limited, to one particular man—*the man who invented dynamite*. Thus, the restrictive clause, ''who invented dynamite'' establishes the specific identity of the word *man.*

Similarly, in the third sentence above, the clause ''which is based on the private ownership of property'' identifies *which* game (of all possible games) is now popular in communist China. It restricts the general word *game* to *one particular* game—*the game which is based on the private ownership of property.*

Since restrictive clauses are necessary to establish the specific identity of the nouns they describe, the following punctuation rule applies:

Restrictive clauses are *not* set off by commas.

In contrast, the clauses in the second and fourth sentences are *not* necessary to identify which particular man established a peace prize or which particular game is now popular in communist China. In these sentences, the man has already been specifically identified as *Alfred Nobel,* and the game has already been specifically identified as *Monopoly*. Since these clauses are *not* restrictive clauses, they are called **nonrestrictive clauses**. Nonrestrictive clauses merely add extra information about the nouns they describe. They serve the same function as appositives and are punctuated in the same way.

Nonrestrictive clauses must be completely set off from the rest of the sentence by commas.

This means that if a nonrestrictive clause is at the *end* of a sentence, it will be *preceded* by a comma. If it is in the *middle* of a sentence, it will be *both preceded and followed* by a comma. (Like appositives, nonrestrictive clauses never occur at the beginning of a sentence since they must follow the noun that they describe.)

The restrictive and nonrestrictive clauses that you have been studying are called **adjective clauses** because, like adjectives, these clauses describe nouns. The words that most frequently introduce adjective clauses are:

that
which
who
whom
whose

Like all clauses, adjective clauses must contain both a subject and a verb. But notice that in adjective clauses *the word that introduces the clause may also be the subject of the clause.*

                     S   V
George is a man *who works hard.*

Or the clause may contain a separate subject:

                     S   V
The picture *that she drew* showed a child's hand.

Adjective clauses, like adverb clauses (see Lesson 9), are used in **complex sentences.** Although these sentences may not seem to be complex at first glance, if you study the sentences above, you will see that each of them has two subjects and two verbs. Also, if the adjective clause, which is the **dependent clause,** is removed from the sentence, a complete independent clause remains.

                              S   V
INDEPENDENT CLAUSE   George is a man

	S V
DEPENDENT CLAUSE	who works hard

	S V
INDEPENDENT CLAUSE	The picture showed a child's hand

	S V
DEPENDENT CLAUSE	that she drew

An adjective clause often occurs in the middle of a sentence since it must follow the noun it describes. When an adjective clause is in the middle of a sentence, part of the independent clause precedes it, and the rest of the independent clause follows it. For example:

S   S   V
Switzerland, *which trains every single adult male for its army,* has avoided

war for centuries.

S   S   V   V
The food *that she likes most* is non-fattening.

A sentence may contain more than one adjective clause. Each clause is punctuated separately. In the following sentences, the first adjective clause is *nonrestrictive* (with commas), and the second clause is *restrictive* (no commas).

The banjo, *which was invented by an American,* uses metal strings *that resonate against a drumhead.*
Death Valley, *which is the lowest point in the United States,* has daytime temperatures *that sometimes reach* 124 *degrees.*

Underline every adjective clause in each of the following sentences, and circle the noun that it describes. Then decide which clauses are restrictive (and do *not* need commas) and which clauses are nonrestrictive (and do need commas). Add the appropriate punctuation.

Note: Although clauses beginning with *who, whom, whose,* or *which* may be either restrictive or nonrestrictive, clauses which begin with *that* are *always* restrictive.

Do you like the present that I gave you?

My father who could repair anything on a car never owned a new car.

She is someone whom Fate has given the looks of a goddess.

The Panama Canal which joins the Atlantic and Pacific Oceans cost the lives of many men.

His uncle Hiram whose wife inherited millions has never done an honest day's work.

Sandra likes men who treat women as equals.

EXERCISE 16A

The essay below includes appositives, parenthetical expressions, direct address, and restrictive and non-restrictive clauses. Add commas and semicolons wherever necessary.

For most people, there is a time which they wish could be forgotten. In my life that time would be my junior year of high school when my relationship with my family went from sweet to sour.

Until my junior year in high school, I made average grades C's and a few B's and was the kind of person who never got into any trouble. I was the oldest girl in my family; I had many responsibilities at home such as looking after my younger brothers, fixing meals, and cleaning the house. I was a daughter who made life easy for her parents.

One night in September of my junior year, that warm relationship with my parents changed radically. It was a Saturday night. I had been asked to go out on my very first date by a boy who had recently moved into our neighborhood. He was seventeen and had the kind of good looks that girls dream about.

My father had already given my fifteen-year-old brother Jack permission to go to the movies as long as he would promise to be home by midnight.

As I went out the door to meet my date my father said, "Sally I want you home at 11:00 P.M."

I could not believe what I had heard. I exploded. I shouted at my father, "Daddy Jack is only fifteen but he can stay out until midnight! I am sixteen and I will stay out as late as I please!"

When my father slapped me I ran out of the house, jumped in my date's car, and stayed out until dawn.

After that I became the kind of daughter who drives her parents crazy. My mother sided with my father. She had always been my friend but now she was my enemy. My grades which had never been high dropped to *D*'s and *F*'s. I took up smoking and went to parties and had fun. Sometimes I would simply not come home after school so that I could avoid my father who couldn't understand what had happened to "his little girl."

Thanks to a school counselor in my senior year I graduated from high school and now I live away from home and support myself. I still believe my father's double standard which made one set of rules for boys and a different set for girls was wrong yet I blame myself for the pain that I put my family through. Although I wish those years could be forgotten I learned a valuable lesson and perhaps I will choose a wiser man for a husband and together we will be wiser parents.

EXERCISE 16B

To the story below, add commas and semicolons wherever they are necessary. This exercise covers all lessons we have studied up to now.

Many hundreds of years ago Britain was ruled by Uther Pendragon. Uther slept with Igraine who was the wife of Gorlois of Cornwall. The illegitimate child of this affair was a son whose birth was hidden from his father the boy was raised in secrecy by Merlin the Magician.

After Uther's death Britain had no king because not one nobleman who tried could withdraw a legendary sword from the stone that held it fast. When the young boy that Merlin had raised pulled out the sword the magician revealed the boy's identity and he was crowned Arthur King of Britain.

Arthur proved to be a noble king and a great warrior. He fought now with another sword Excalibur which had been given to him by the mysterious Lady of the Lake. At his main castle Camelot Arthur established the Knights of the Round Table a group of warriors who served Arthur against the forces of evil that wanted to tyrannize the kingdom. Among Arthur's famous knights were Sir Tristan, Sir Galahad, Sir Gawain, and Sir Launcelot.

Although Launcelot was Arthur's closest friend he could not keep from falling in love with Arthur's queen the lovely Guenivere. She returned Launcelot's love and they betrayed Arthur again and again. Arthur learned of their infidelity but because he loved them both and because the penalty for her infidelity was death he suffered in silence. However Arthur's enemies who wanted to destroy the noble reign of him and his queen brought Guenivere's adultery out in the open. She would have been burned at the stake but when a mysterious knight appeared who successfully fought for her honor her life was spared.

Arthur's greatest enemies were his sister Morgan Le Fey and her son Mordred. They plotted and plotted to kill him. After many years Arthur at last killed Mordred in battle but as he died Mordred was able to give Arthur a wound that would kill him also.

The body of Arthur was borne away to the isle of Avalon where it will stay until its wounds are magically healed. Then as the story goes Arthur will return to rule Britain again. For this reason he is called the Once and Future King.

EXERCISE 16C

Part One   Construct complex sentences of your own using the words listed below to form *restrictive* clauses. Underline the adjective clause in each of your sentences, and circle the noun it describes.

1. that: _____

_____

2. who: _____

_____

3. which: _____

_____

4. whose: _____

_____

Part Two   Construct complex sentences of your own using the words listed below to form *nonrestrictive* clauses. Underline the adjective clause in each of your sentences, and circle the noun it describes. Use appropriate punctuation.

5. which: _____

_____

6. who: _____

_____

7. whose: _____

_____

8. whom: _____

_____

Part Three Underline the adjective clauses in the following sentences, and circle the word which each clause describes. If the clause is nonrestrictive, add the necessary punctuation. If the clause is restrictive, the sentence needs no additional punctuation, so label it *C* for *correct.*

9. Humans need a system of time that allows them to record past events and to plan for the future.

10. However, since time systems are based on natural events like the movements of heavenly bodies, Mother Nature has not made such systems easy to create.

11. For example, the time period that we call a *year* is based on the earth's orbit around the sun.

12. If this orbit took a convenient number of days, like an even 100 days, it would be easy to make a calendar.

13. But the time that it takes earth to orbit the sun is not at all convenient since it adds up to 365 days + 5 hours + 48 minutes + 46 seconds.

14. Because a year cannot be exactly divided by days, we must add one day every fourth year which is called a *leap year.*

15. In a leap year, the short month of February which normally has twenty-eight days must add one day.

16. You know the reason, don't you, for having five other months that have thirty days and six other months that have thirty-one days?

17

Items in a Series and Dates and Addresses

A **series** consists of *three or more* related items. Commas are placed between each item in a series in order to separate the items from each other. The final comma before the conjunction is optional.

Jogging, dancing, and singing are three activities she loves.

or

Jogging, dancing and singing are three activities she loves.

If *every* item in a series is joined by a conjunction (*and, or,* or *nor*), no commas are needed since the conjunctions keep the individual items separated. This type of construction is used only when the writer wishes to place particular emphasis on the number of items in the series.

The cost of college may include tuition and books and transportation.

If a date or an address consists of more than one item, a comma is used after each part of the date or the address, *including a comma after the last item.* (If the last item in the series is also the last word in the sentence, only a period follows it.) Notice that this punctuation rule differs from the rule used for punctuating an ordinary series.

February 12, 1809, was the birthday of Abraham Lincoln.

The name of a month and the number of the day (February 12) are considered a single item and are separated from the year by a comma. However, notice that a comma also *follows* 1809, which is the last item in the date.

The old Chisholm Trail from San Antonio, Texas, to Abilene, Kansas, was used to move cattle from the range to railroad depots.

Notice the commas after "Texas" and "Kansas." These commas are used in addition to the commas that separate the names of the cities from the names of the states.

If a date or an address consists of only a single item, no comma is necessary.

February 14 is Valentine's Day.
I have lived in both Michigan and California.

A comma is not used before a Zip Code number.

The mailing address for Hollywood is Los Angeles, California 90028.

Punctuate the following sentences:

Every mini-mall in the neighborhood has a frozen yogurt shop a Chinese restaurant and a VCR store.

His professor lectured answered questions and gave the test.

If you drive fifty-five miles per hour, you can go from Long Island New York to Los Angeles California in six or seven days.

Louella wants ham with gravy and coffee with cream.

Jackie resides at 904 Adams Street Mercer Idaho 70413.

EXERCISE 17A

Add commas to the following sentences wherever they are needed. If a sentence needs no additional punctuation, label it *C* for *correct*. This exercise covers only the punctuation of items in a series and dates and addresses.

1. My cousin likes Wilmington North Carolina more than Chicago.

2. When our diet was finished, we ordered pie with ice cream and coffee with sugar.

3. Geraldo's car is very old very beautiful and very fast. (Notice that adjectives, like nouns, may be in a series.)

4. The plane made stops in Albuquerque New Mexico and Kansas City Kansas before flying on to Newark New Jersey.

5. Tanya's parents celebrate their silver wedding anniversary on the third of May.

6. Sam launched his plane watched it rise slowly toward the heavens and then stared as it began to dive straight down. (Notice that verbs, like nouns, may be in a series.)

7. Maria's best friends in school were Betty Sobel Mark Lassiter and Rodney Rodriquez.

8. The lecture covered the causes of the problem the long-term effects of the problem and some suggestions for a solution.

9. Is April Fool's Day on April 1 or on April 31?

10. Send the larger package to 9492 West Jefferson Avenue Apartment 14D Yakima WA 98908.

11. May 27 1928 is the day my grandmother was born.

12. Stamp collecting butterfly collecting baseball card collecting and man collecting are Janice's hobbies.

13. Bradley sent cards to his friend Terry his sister Marjorie his Uncle Nathan and his boss.

14. The subscription ran from June 9 to January 9.

EXERCISE 17B

Add semicolons and commas wherever they are necessary in the following letter. This exercise covers all of the lessons on punctuation that we have studied.

November 19 1989

Mr. Vernon Hardison

Bell-Pak Corporation

911 Colson Boulevard Smithville Ohio

Dear Mr. Hardison:

On September 3 of last month I ordered from your firm nineteen dozen Size 12 cartons forty dozen Size 8 cartons and sixteen dozen Size 5 cartons. I wished to prepay my order so I enclosed a check for the full amount of the order and for the shipping and handling fee the check totalled $2187.00. This order last month was exactly like orders I placed with your firm a year ago on September 5 1988 in September of 1987 and in September of 1986.

The orders that I placed with you in 1986 1987 and 1988 arrived within a week of the date ordered and included all the items I had asked for. I was billed correctly for the items in the order. However the order that I made just a month ago was completely botched by your firm. I asked to have it sent as quickly as possible. Instead of arriving around November 25 1989 when I expected it it did not arrive until December 17 1989 after it was too late for me to use the items for my Christmas sale.

Your firm also botched the delivery address. The order arrived at 7:00 P.M. to our store at 7642 Wilson Avenue Smithville Pennsylvania which is our retail outlet but I clearly told your salesperson to deliver the order to our Ohio warehouse which is located three miles away at 683 Royton Street Smithville Ohio.

Furthermore instead of getting the items that I ordered in the quantities that I requested, this is what arrived: twelve dozen Size 7 cartons eight dozen Size 2 cartons and five dozen Size 18 cartons!

I am returning all the merchandise to you C.O.D. as soon as possible and I expect a full refund. If your insurance covers such mistakes I will be happy to aid you in filing a claim to compensate me for the sales that I lost because of this bungled order.

I know that things are always extra busy before Christmas and that it's confusing for your people when a town straddles the borders of two states but you will agree won't you that special care is called for when you are dealing with a repeat order from a valued customer like me.

Sincerely,

I. M. Opsett

Review of Punctuation that "Sets Off" or Separates

Add commas and semicolons (no periods) to the following sentences wherever they are necessary.

Once upon a time, a small village owned a wonderful creature a golden goose. The villagers treasured this goose because she laid eggs that were made of gold. These gold eggs could be traded for things that the villagers needed or the gold could be made into beautiful jewelry that all the villagers wore. Of course the villagers took good care of this goose which made their lives so content. But one villager a selfish man was not content with having only a share of the gold. On a dark night he crept to where the goose was kept a pen in the heart of the village. His mind was full of dreams of himself as the richest man in the whole word. He killed the goose and cut her open to find all her gold eggs. However not a single egg did he find in the dead goose and so he ran away into the darkness to leave his village behind forever.

This old fable has not lost its meaning. Today the world is one community a single large village. Some very important things belong to all of us in the same way that the goose belonged to the whole village. The air that we need for life belongs to all of us. The seas of the earth which give us food to eat and rain to water our earth and beaches to enjoy belong to all of us. Many things belong to all of us don't they and to our children yet unborn.

A second meaning we may derive from the fable is the danger of ignorance about how things work. The selfish man of the village thought that the goose would be full of eggs, but of course it wasn't. The goose could not be brought back to life after the man's mistake. We humans have already completely eliminated some living forms for example we have killed all of the passenger pigeons for their feathers. Many other life forms like whales are endangered almost to the point of extinction. We may at this very moment be damaging our soil and oceans and atmosphere in ways we can never repair.

The final meaning of the fable is the hardest for each of us to admit. Each of us sometimes dreams, *"It would be nice wouldn't it to have all those gold eggs inside that goose for myself?"*

PRONOUN
USAGE

18

Subject, Object, and Possessive Pronouns

Pronouns are words that are used to refer to persons, places, things, and ideas without repeating their names. In other words, pronouns are used in place of nouns. For example, rather than saying "Mark bought a new pen only yesterday, but Mark has already lost the pen," you can say, "Mark bought a new pen only yesterday, but *he* has already lost *it*." In this sentence, the pronoun *he* replaces *Mark*, and the pronoun *it* replaces *pen*. The noun that the pronoun replaces is called the **antecedent** (Latin for "to go before") of the pronoun.

There are several different kinds of pronouns, but in this lesson you will be studying only **subject pronouns, object pronouns,** and **possessive pronouns**.

Singular Pronouns	*Subject*	*Object*	*Possessive*
	I	me	my, mine
	you	you	your, yours
	he	him	his
	she	her	her, hers
	it	it	its

Plural Pronouns	*Subject*	*Object*	*Possessive*
	we	us	our, ours
	you	you	your, yours
	they	them	their, theirs

As their name suggests, **subject pronouns** are used as the *subject* of a sentence or a clause. For example:

She is a vice-president at General Dynamics.
They live in the apartment upstairs.

In *formal* speech and writing, subject pronouns are also used after forms of the verb *be,* as in:

That is *he* at the door.
It is *I.*
If I were *she,* I'd take the job.

In formal speech and writing, subject pronouns are used after forms of the verb *be* because they refer to the *same* thing or person as the subject.

That = he at the door.
It = I.
If I *= she,* I'd take the job.

However, in *informal* speech, many people would use object pronouns in the sentences below.

That is (or *That's*) *him* at the door.
It is (or *It's*) *me.*
If I were *her,* I'd take the job.

Whether you choose to say "it is I" or "it is me" depends upon the circumstances. If you are taking an English test or writing a formal essay, using subject pronouns after forms of *be* is appropriate and expected. But if you are speaking casually with a friend, "it is I" may sound artificial, and the informal "it is me" might be more suitable.

In this unit, you will be studying both grammar and usage. Try to keep clear in your mind those situations in which you have a choice between formal and informal constructions (usage) and those situations in which only one pronoun form is correct at all times (grammar).

"It is *she*" versus "It is *her*" = usage.
"Al and *I* are here" versus "Al and *me* are here" = grammar.

Object pronouns are used as objects of prepositions, as direct objects, and as indirect objects.

You will remember that the noun or pronoun in a prepositional phrase is called the **object of the preposition.** That is why an object pronoun replaces the noun. For example:

The report was sent to *Marie*.
The report was sent to *her*.
The cheerleader yelled at the *fans*.
The cheerleader yelled at *them*.

Object pronouns are also used as direct objects. A **direct object** is the word that *receives* the action of the verb and, with very few exceptions, follows the verb, often as the next word.

The teacher tested the *students*.
   (subject)   (direct object)

The teacher tested *them*.

She liked *Frank* immediately.
(subject)   (direct object)

She liked *him* immediately.

Another way in which object pronouns are used is as indirect objects. An **indirect object** is the person or thing *to whom* or *for whom* something is done.

They awarded the *winner* a prize.
(subject)   (indirect   (direct
                         object)   object)

They awarded *her* a prize.

The previous sentence is another way of saying, "They awarded a prize *to her*."

Lonnie bought his *sister* a new album.
(subject) (indirect (direct
     object) object)

Lonnie bought *her* a new album.

The previous sentence is another way of saying, "Lonnie bought a new album *for her*."

Possessive pronouns are used to show ownership.

The tiger licked *its* paw.
The men shaved *their* beards after the contest.

Very few people make pronoun errors when there is only one subject or one object in a sentence. For example, no native speaker of English would say, "Me am here" instead of "I am here." However, people often do make mistakes when two subjects or two objects are paired up in a sentence. For example, which of the following two sentences is grammatically correct?

Mrs. Jones invited my husband and *me* to her party.
Mrs. Jones invited my husband and *I* to her party.

To determine the correct pronoun in this kind of "double" construction, split the sentence in two like this:

1. Mrs. Jones invited my husband to her party.
2. Mrs. Jones invited (me, I) to her party.

As you can tell after you have split the sentence in two, it would be incorrect to say "Mrs. Jones invited *I* to her party." The correct pronoun is *me,* which is the direct object of the verb *invited.* Therefore, the whole sentence should read:

Mrs. Jones invited my husband and *me* to her party.

Which of the following two sentences is correct?

Janet mailed Lorne and *I* the package.
Janet mailed Lorne and *me* the package.

Again, split the sentences in two.

1. Janet mailed Lorne the package.
2. Janet mailed (I, me) the package.

Now, which pronoun is correct?

Another very common pronoun error is using subject pronouns instead of object pronouns after prepositions. The object of a preposition must be an *object* pronoun. Which of the following two sentences is correct?

The teacher returned the test to Ken and *I.*
The teacher returned the test to Ken and *me.*

If you split the sentence in two, you have:

1. The teacher returned the test to Ken.
2. The teacher returned the test to (I, me).

The correct pronoun is *me,* which is the object of the preposition *to.* Therefore, the correct sentence is:

The teacher returned the test to Ken and *me.*

It is extremely important that you do not decide which pronoun to use simply on the basis of what "sounds better" *unless you split the sentence in two first.* To many people, "Mrs. Jones invited my husband and *I* to her party" sounds more "correct" than "Mrs. Jones invited my husband and *me* to her party"; yet, as you have seen, *me* is actually the correct pronoun.

Another example of choosing an incorrect pronoun because it "sounds better" is the frequent misuse of the subject pronoun *I* after the preposition *between.* As you already know, the object of a preposition must be an *object* pronoun. Therefore, it is always incorrect to say 'between you and *I.*" The *correct* construction is "between you and *me.*"

Circle the pronoun that correctly completes each of the following sentences.

It should be divided between you and (I, me).

They warned our friends and (we, us) about prowlers.

My uncle and (he, him) ride the same bus.

The coach gave the team and (I, me) another chance.

The award is for you and (she, her).

Occasionally you may use constructions like the following:

Does the new law concern *us women*?
We voters must elect good leaders.

To determine whether the sentence requires a subject or an object pronoun, see which pronoun would be correct if the pronoun appeared in the sentence by itself rather than being followed by a noun.

Does the new law concern (us, we) women? =
Does the new law concern (we, us)?
(We, us) voters must elect responsible candidates. =
(We, us) must elect responsible candidates.
The correct pronouns are *us* women and *we* voters.

Circle the pronoun that correctly completes each of the following sentences.

It is not for (we, us) relatives to settle the argument.

(We, us) club members should publish a newsletter.

EXERCISE 18A

The first part of this exercise is intended for a quick review of subject and object pronouns. Reverse each sentence so that the subject pronoun becomes the object and the object pronoun becomes the subject.

Example: *I* waited for *them.*
Answer: *They* waited for *me.*

1. *She* wrote *him* last month.

2. *He* gave *them* too much time.

3. *They* sent the packages to *him.*

4. *You* relied on *us* for support.

5. *I* respected *her* so much.

6. *We* baked *him* a cake.

7. *They* wrote one essay for *her* each week.

8. *We* stalked *it* through the underbrush.

Circle the pronoun that correctly completes each sentence. Remember to split the sentence if it contains a "double" construction. Apply the rules of formal English usage.

9. John and (them, they) liked the same foods.

10. It was (he, him) in the darkness.

11. Melissa and (she, her) were on the same team.

12. That was already decided by the other members and (I, me).

13. The woman with the most votes and (she, her) were the new officers.

14. (We, us) oldtimers ought to give the new director a chance.

15. The family was pleased with (they, them) and their choice.

16. The leftovers were divided between Carlos and (he, him).

17. Can you see who sent this to Sam and (her, she)?

18. The decision was made by (we, us) former captains.

19. Lorraine and (her, she) get along well.

20. Was it (they, them) outside the window?

EXERCISE 18B

Some of the following sentences contain pronoun errors. Cross out the incorrect pronouns, and write in the correct forms. If a sentence contains no pronoun errors, label it *C* for *correct*. Apply the rules of formal English usage.

1. Did you get the assignment for Jill and me?

2. You disappointed Larry and they when you left early.

3. Us psychology majors have a meeting at 11:00.

4. The program appealed to Darryl and them.

5. The car barely missed Walter and us.

6. With them and me on your team, we'll have a good game.

7. You and her ought to try Mr. Wilson's class.

8. Last year our opponents and us had a post-game party.

9. We borrowers of library books were sent a final notice.

10. You can lean on Warner or I for assistance.

11. The second ones to reach the finals were Jackie and me.

12. Both her uncle and her know the trail to the river.

13. If us adults don't set a good example, what can we expect?

14. They arrested both Wilkes and him after the raid.

15. Reba has asked to present a case for all of us petitioners at the meeting.

16. She wanted Art and I to go with her.

17. Surely between you and I, we can solve this problem.

18. Their tenants and them can't get along.

19. I saw Bud talking to her last night.

20. The bill was passed through Congress by the hard work of Willard Reese and them.

EXERCISE 18C

Part One   Give the following sentences two subjects by adding a subject pronoun to each sentence. *Use a different pronoun for each sentence.* Apply the rules of formal English usage. The first sentence has been done as an example.

        and she
1. Those people upstairs ∧ are neighbors.

2. The women are good workers.

3. The owner of the shop left early.

4. The man in the truck crashed.

5. Melissa took art classes last year.

6. His friend from work bought a high-powered telescope.

7. The three snakes met in the middle of the pond.

Part Two   Give the following sentences two objects by adding an object pronoun to each sentence. *Use a different object pronoun for each sentence.* Apply the rules of formal English usage. The first sentence has been done as an example.

        and him
8. She wrote Terri ∧ last week.

9. He commutes with Harry to the new plant.

10. The painting was completed by Arnold.

11. Corey works for Sue.

12. That typist finished after Amanda.

13. Their best runner outran Mario.

14. We left without Sally.

15. The President received a message concerning the Ambassador.

16. The ball rolled toward Isaac.

19

Pronouns in Comparisons and Pronouns with -self, -selves

Using Pronouns in Comparisons

In speech and in writing, we often compare two people or two things with each other. For example:

Marcia is wiser than *I* am.
The mechanic charged *Ike* more than he charged *me*.

In the sentences above, it is easy to tell whether a subject pronoun or an object pronoun should be used in each comparison. In the first sentence, the subject pronoun *I* is correct because it would be clearly ungrammatical to say that "Marcia is wiser than *me* am." In the second sentence, the object pronoun *me* is correct because you would not say that "The mechanic charged Ike more than he charged *I*."

However, people usually do not write out their comparisons completely. They use a shortened form instead. For example:

Tammy cooks better than *I.*
The film impressed *Don* more than *me.*   ·

In these cases, it is possible to determine which pronoun is correct by mentally filling in the words that have been left out of the comparison.

Tammy cooks better than I (do).
The film impressed Don more than (it impressed) me.

Fill in the missing words to determine which pronouns are correct in the following sentences.

My co-worker deserves more praise than (I, me).

Making good grades is harder for Ed than (I, me).

His family reads less than (we, us).

The news shocked you more than (he, him).

When you fill in the missing words, the correct comparisons are:

My co-worker deserves more praise than *I* (do).
Making good grades is harder for Ed than (it is for) *me.*
His family reads less than *we* (do).
The news shocked you more than (it shocked) *him.*

In *informal* usage, you often hear people use object pronouns instead of subject pronouns in comparisons. (For example, "He's taller than me" instead of "He's taller than I.") However, these forms are generally considered inappropriate in writing and formal speech. You should be especially careful in situations where the wrong pronoun can change the meaning of the entire sentence. For example, "Mary danced with George more than *I* (danced with him)" does not mean the same thing as "Mary danced with George more than (she danced with) *me.*" In addition, using the wrong pronoun can sometimes lead to unintentionally ridiculous sentences, such as:

My husband likes cake more than me.

Unless the husband happens to like food more than he likes his wife, the correct pronoun would be:

My husband likes cake more than *I* (do).

(Note: The conjunction *than,* which is used in comparisons, should not be confused with the adverb *then.*)

Avoiding Doubled Subjects

Do not "double," or repeat, the subject of a sentence by repeating the noun in its pronoun form.

INCORRECT	My friend, she never pays attention.
CORRECT	My friend never pays attention.
INCORRECT	Those new models, they break down easily.
CORRECT	Those new models break down easily.

Pronouns with -self, -selves

Some pronouns end in *-self* or *-selves:*

Singular	*Plural*
myself	ourselves
yourself	yourselves
himself	themselves
herself	
itself	

These pronouns can be used in two ways. They can be reflexive pronouns. **Reflexive pronouns** are used when the object of the verb or the object of the preposition is the same person or thing as the subject. For example:

I touched *myself.* (myself = I)
Greg teaches *himself.* (himself = Greg)
Helen could look at *herself.* (herself = Helen)

Or they may be used for *emphasis.*

The judge *herself* said they were innocent.
Did you build the whole house *yourself?*
We *ourselves* were responsible for the crash.

Notice that the singular forms of reflexive pronouns end in *self,* and the plural forms end in *selves.* In standard English, there are no such forms as *hisself, ourselfs, theirselfs,* or *themselfs.* These forms are considered nonstandard in both speech and writing and should be avoided unless you are using a dialect, as in a short story, in which they are the customary forms.

In formal English, the reflexive pronoun *myself* is not used in place of a subject or an object pronoun.

INCORRECT   Jack and *myself* will meet you at 8:00.
CORRECT   Jack and *I* will meet you at 8:00.
INCORRECT   This present is for Alice and *myself.*
CORRECT   This present is for Alice and *me.*

Myself is sometimes used as a subject or an object pronoun in informal usage, but even in these cases the use of the correct subject or object pronoun is preferred. Referring to yourself as *myself* rather than as *I* or *me* does *not* make you sound more polite or more modest.

EXERCISE 19A

Circle the pronoun that most logically and correctly completes each sentence. Apply the rules of formal English usage.

1. Are Leila and (they, them) good friends?

2. Either Bonita or (I, myself) will take you.

3. They are both tall, but she is stronger than (he, him).

4. Ship the box to Sam or (I, me).

5. They speak better English than (we, us).

6. The judge gave John a longer sentence than (her, she).

7. They have known us longer than (he, him).

8. The ugliest couple in the contest is she and (I, myself).

9. We've been living here longer than (they, them).

10. Are the mayor and (they, them) still squabbling over money?

11. Ronnie or (me, I) will meet your plane.

12. Although neither of them is working, he spends much more than (her, she).

13. Lonnie and (myself, I) took photos of the capitol.

14. This picture shows three veterans and (myself, me).

15. His sweetheart likes to dance more than (him, he).

16. Typing rapidly is easier for Wanda than for (I, me).

17. The disaster shocked the family more than (she, her).

18. We reacted angrily to lies about the team and (us, ourselves).

19. They campaigned hard and voted for (theirselves, themselves).

20. The coach for the junior varsity team chose the player with less experience than (I, me).

EXERCISE 19B

In the essay below cross out the pronoun errors and replace them with the correct forms. This exercise covers this lesson and the previous lesson.

My older sister had a much more successful passage through adolescence than me. She attended all four years of high school at Lincoln High School in Chicago. I went to Lincoln for two years, but then my father, he decided to move our family to what he called a healthier environment.

I was then a very shy person. At Lincoln High in Chicago it took me almost a year to make friends. In my science class were a girl and a boy who were even shyer than me. After they and I fouled up a chemistry experiment, the three of us became close friends. By the end of my sophomore year, I was going to games and dances and enjoying myself in high school.

One night in the spring of my sophomore year, my dad said at the dinner table, ''Well, kids, your mom and me have made a big decision. Us Smiths are all going to move ourselves off to the country to a small town in Virginia.''

That was it. No discussion, no warning. I was crushed, but my sister, she didn't care because she was going to college anyway.

That summer we moved to the small town of Madison, Virginia, population 872, and I became a shy person all over again.

At Madison High there were three strikes against me. I was a stranger, I was a "city girl," and, worst of all, I was a "Yankee" who talked funny. Many of our neighbors were friendly enough to our family, but just between you and I, high school girls can be very cruel to someone who is not part of "their gang." I spent most of my time by myself being miserable and wishing my friends from Chicago and I were back together.

On Halloween night of my senior year, a strange thing happened. My parents and me were at the grocery store, and Rob Tilley was the checker. He was one of the brains in the senior class, but also a person who liked to go his own way. And his folks owned the only grocery store in town. As he handed me our bag of groceries, he looked me right in the eye and said, "Well, Yankee girl, how would it be if you and I went to the dance after I get off work?"

From that night on the feelings between him and me grew so strong that we ran off in the spring to get married. Now I'm commuting to the local community college, and expecting my first child. My path through adolescence was rocky, but it ended very happily.

20

Agreement of Pronouns with Their Antecedents

Agreement in Number

Like nouns, pronouns may be either singular or plural, depending upon whether they refer to one or to more than one person or thing. Following are the subject, object, and possessive pronouns you have learned, divided into singular and plural categories.

Singular Pronouns	*Subject*	*Object*	*Possessive*
	I	me	my, mine
	you	you	your, yours
	he	him	his
	she	her	her, hers
	it	it	its

Plural Pronouns	*Subject*	*Object*	*Possessive*
	we	us	our, ours
	you	you	your, yours
	they	them	their, theirs

Just as a subject must agree in number with its verb, a pronoun must agree in number with its **antecedent.** (The antecedent, you will remember, is the noun to which the pronoun refers.) In other words, if the antecedent is *singular,* the pronoun must be *singular.* If the antecedent is *plural,* the pronoun must be *plural.*

Study the following sentences, in which both the pronouns and their antecedents have been italicized.

> After the *man* wrote the letter, *he* mailed it.
> After the *men* wrote the letter, *they* mailed it.

Obviously, few people would make pronoun agreement errors in the above sentences since *man* is clearly singular, and *men* is clearly plural. However, people often make pronoun agreement errors in cases like the following:

INCORRECT   A *driver* should reduce *their* speed in bad weather.
CORRECT   A *driver* should reduce *his* speed in bad weather.

Since drivers include females as well as males, it would be equally correct to say:

> A driver should reduce *her* speed in bad weather.
> A driver should reduce *his* or *her* speed in bad weather.

For a more detailed discussion of the *his or her* construction, see the section on "Avoiding Sexist Language" on page 212.

Notice the differences in these sentences.

INCORRECT   Each *person* is entitled to *their* own locker.
CORRECT   Each *person* is entitled to *his* own locker.

What causes people to make mistakes like these? The mistakes may occur because when a writer describes a *driver,* he or she is thinking of drivers (plural) in general. Similarly, a writer may think of a *person* as people in general. Nevertheless, since *driver* and *person* are singular nouns, they must be used with singular pronouns.

Notice that if several pronouns refer to the same antecedent, *all* of the pronouns must agree in number with that antecedent.

If *Nancy* expects higher grades, *she* should do all *her* work.
When the *tourists* leave, *they* take *their* memories with *them.*

Another common pronoun agreement error involves **indefinite pronouns.**
As you learned in Lesson 7 on subject−verb agreement (p. 71), indefinite pronouns are *singular* and require *singular* verbs. (For example, "Everyone *is*
here," *not* "Everyone *are* here.") Similarly, when indefinite pronouns are used
as antecedents, they require *singular* subject, object, and possessive pronouns.
The following words are singular indefinite pronouns.

anybody, anyone, anything
each, each one
either, neither
everybody, everyone, everything
nobody, no one, nothing
somebody, someone, something

Notice the use of singular pronouns with these words.

Everyone did as he pleased.
Somebody has forgotten *her* shawl.
Either of the choices has *its* disadvantages.

In informal spoken English, plural pronouns are often used with indefinite
pronoun antecedents. However, this construction is generally not considered
appropriate in formal speech or writing.

INFORMAL   *Somebody* wants *their* lawyer to phone *them.*
  FORMAL   *Somebody* wants *his* lawyer to phone *him.*

In some sentences, an indefinite pronoun is so clearly plural in meaning
that a singular pronoun sounds awkward with it. For example:

Everyone on this block must be wealthy because he drives a Cadillac or
a Mercedes.

A better wording for this sentence would be:

All the people on this block must be wealthy because they all drive a Cadillac or a Mercedes.

Avoiding Sexist Language

Although the matching of singular pronouns with singular antecedents is a grammatical problem, a usage problem may occur if the antecedent of a singular pronoun refers to both sexes. In the past, singular masculine pronouns were used to refer to antecedents such as *person* or *driver* even if these antecedents included women as well as men. Now, many writers prefer to use forms that include both sexes, such as *he or she* or *his or her* in order to avoid excluding females.

Every student should turn his or her papers in on time.
If anyone has seen the missing child, he or she should call the police immediately.

A simpler way is to make both the pronoun and its antecedent plural.

All *students* should turn in *their* papers on time.

Avoiding sexist language is a problem of usage, not of grammar. In order to simplify the rules for you while you are still studying grammar, most of the exercises in this unit will offer you the choice between one singular pronoun (either masculine or feminine) and one plural pronoun. For example:

Everyone should do (her, their) best on the job.
Each parent is responsible for (his, their) own children.

Which pronouns would be correct in the following sentences according to the rules of formal English usage?

If a person wants to lose weight, (he, they) should eat less and exercise more.
A surgeon may spend seven or eight hours on (her, their) feet during a complex operation.
Anyone who knows the answer should raise (their, his) hand.
A good pilot knows (their, her) airplane.
Each of the groups has (its, their) instructions.

Agreement in Person

In grammar, pronouns are classified into groups called **persons. First person** refers to the person who is speaking. **Second person** is the person being spoken to. **Third person** is the person or thing being spoken about. Below is a chart of subject pronouns grouped according to person.

	Singular	*Plural*
first person	I	we
second person	you	you
third person	he, she, it	they

All nouns are considered third person (either singular or plural) because nouns can be replaced by third-person pronouns (for example, *Bob* = *he; a book* = *it; apples* = *they*).

Just as a pronoun and its antecedent must agree in number, they must also agree in person. Agreement in person usually becomes a problem when the second-person pronoun *you* is incorrectly used with a third-person antecedent. Study the following examples.

INCORRECT If *anyone* is allergic to pollen, *you* should avoid the source.
CORRECT If *anyone* is allergic to pollen, *he* should avoid the source.
INCORRECT When *voters* go to the polls, *you* should receive your ballot stub.
CORRECT When *voters* go to the polls, *they* should receive their ballot stubs.

This type of mistake is called a **shift in person** and is considered a serious grammatical error.

In addition to avoiding shifts in person within individual sentences, you should try to be consistent in your use of person when you are writing essays. In general, an entire essay is written in the same person. If, for example, you are writing an essay about the special problems faced by students who work full-time, you will probably use either the first or the third person. You should avoid shifts into the second person (*you*) since *you* refers to the reader of your paper and not to the students you are writing about.

INCORRECT	*Students* who take too many units must often drop classes later in the semester. When *you* register, *you* should plan realistically for the amount of time *you* can allocate to *your* classes and homework.
CORRECT	*Students* who take too many units must often drop classes during the semester. When *they* register, *they* should plan realistically for the amount of time *they* can allocate to *their* classes and homework.

Circle the pronoun that correctly completes each sentence.

Please listen carefully; (your, his, their) full attention is required.

Many states now have no-fault auto insurance for all drivers so that (you, he, they) do not need to go to court to settle (your, his, their) accident claims.

If a person wants to run for office, (they, you, she) must be known to the voters.

EXERCISE 20A

Circle the pronouns that correctly complete each sentence. Apply the rules of formal English usage.

1. After a trainee is promoted, (she, you) will get a raise.

2. Either the manager or the assistant manager will see you in (his, their) office.

3. After Willy and (her, she) were married, they became better friends.

4. The club is supported entirely by the members (theirselves, themselves).

5. She was selected much later than (they, them).

6. After consumers watch these ads, (you, they) will buy a million Whoopdoodles.

7. Whenever I study more than (him, he), I make a higher score.

8. Anybody in the group may voice (her, their) opinion.

9. No one who saw the film was as angry as (he, him).

10. (She, Her) and I have taken many of the same classes.

11. Please take the remaining food and divide it between the boys in the back room and (I, me).

12. Either of the companies could be in trouble by ignoring (their, its) competition.

13. Pregnant women who work outside the home are often asked to resign or are given job assignments that will make them want to quit; if (they, you) are employed, (you, they) should know what rights (they, you) have under the law.

EXERCISE 20B

If a sentence contains an error in pronoun usage, cross out the incorrect pronoun, and write in the correct form. Some sentences contain more than one error. If a sentence contains no pronoun errors, label it *C* for *correct*. Apply the rules of formal English usage.

1. Either Alana or Bessie has left her purse behind.

2. He has to pick hisself up and go back to work.

3. Any one of the women will let you use their key.

4. Whenever people are faced with sudden change, they may react unpredictably.

5. She knew that Debbie had assembled her evidence carefully.

6. Weldon finished two seconds sooner than us.

7. Has anyone finished the first draft of her essay?

8. All winners should report to the judges' table to pick up your prizes.

9. I'm sure that either you or them will know the answer.

10. The speakers were her and her sister.

11. When a cardholder has a complaint, they should call this number.

12. The representative from Iowa was much angrier than him.

13. When Eustace looked up the word, he found it on the last page.

14. That argument was easier for the prosecutor than them.

EXERCISE 20C

Part One Complete the following sentences by adding a pronoun. Be sure your choice of pronoun agrees in number with its antecedent. Apply the rules of formal English usage. The first sentence has been done as an example.

1. Each member of the square provided _____*her*_____ own lunch.

2. My cousins get _____ red hair from their mother.

3. Before a voter votes, _____ must be a registered voter.

4. Everybody at the meeting had _____ own proposal for consideration.

5. Because Jason and Elizabeth are old friends, _____ share many memories.

6. Those people who wish to take this class must pay _____ lab fees during registration.

7. My brother had to pass an examination before receiving _____ new job classification.

8. Each book is placed in the library according to _____ call number.

9. Somebody broke into the safe but did not leave _____ fingerprints.

10. Every ticketholder should save _____ stub.

11. The Hodgsons and _____ will go together.

12. My uncle Rex sent me more than _____.

Part Two   For each sentence below, write a second sentence containing at least two pronouns that refer to nouns or pronouns in the first sentence. Circle these pronouns. Employ formal usage. The first pair of sentences has been done as an example.

1. My sister is taking four college classes. *(She) likes (her) math* _____

class best although (she) finds all of (them) interesting. _____

2. Any member may make a motion. _____

_____

_____

3. Your job is to file these cards according to each woman's last name.

_____

_____

_____

4. Those ticketholders who purchased before July 15 have first choice

of seats. _____

_____

_____

5. Someone left these books at the Lost and Found. _____

_____

_____

6. Drivers should be very careful on that part of the highway. _____

_____

_____

21

Order of Pronouns and Spelling of Possessives

Order of Pronouns

When you are referring to someone else and to yourself in the same sentence, mention the other person's name (or the pronoun that replaces the name) before you mention your own.

INCORRECT	*I* and Joan like to study together.
CORRECT	Joan and *I* like to study together.
INCORRECT	The class listened to *me* and him.
CORRECT	The class listened to him and *me*.

The construction is actually not a rule of grammar; rather, it is considered a matter of courtesy.

Possessive Pronouns

Here is a list of possessive pronouns that you have already studied. This time, look carefully at how they are spelled and punctuated.

	Singular	*Plural*
first person	my, mine	our, ours
second person	your, yours	your, yours
third person	his	their, theirs
	her, hers	
	its	

Possessive pronouns do *not* contain apostrophes.

INCORRECT	That idea was *her's.*
CORRECT	That idea was *hers.*

Be especially careful not to confuse the possessive pronoun *its* with the contraction *it's* (it is).

INCORRECT	The movie pleased *it's* audience.
CORRECT	The movie pleased *its* audience.

Another source of confusion is the apostrophe which indicates the omitted letters in contractions. For example, the apostrophe in *don't* represents the missing *o* from **do not.** Some contractions of pronouns and verbs have the same pronunciations as certain possessive pronouns. These pairs of words sound alike but differ in meaning. Don't confuse them in your writing.

who's–whose
    Who's he? = *Who is* he?
    Whose seat is this? (possessive)
you're–your
    You're the winner. = *You are* the winner.
    It is *your* turn. (possessive)
they're–their
    They're leaving. = *They are* leaving.
    Their entry was selected. (possessive)

Circle the pronoun that correctly completes each sentence.

This coin is (yours, your's).

(Whose, Who's) your friend?

The bank just raised (its, it's) fees.

I don't know (whose, who's) car that is.

(Your, You're) luck has run out.

The new baby is (theirs, their's).

A final note: When you do pronoun exercises, or when you use pronouns in your own writing, remember to apply the rules. If you rely only on what "sounds right," your ear will usually supply only those pronouns that are appropriate in *informal* English.

EXERCISE 21A

If a sentence contains an error in pronoun usage, cross out the incorrect pronoun, and write in the correct form. Some sentences may contain more than one error. If a sentence contains no pronoun errors, label it *C* for *correct.* Apply the rules of formal English usage.

1. We team members won our heat in the race.

2. For that type of report use a source who's authority is unquestionable.

3. The application should always come from the applicant hisself.

4. The coach sent me and Jenny to the showers.

5. If its all right with you, I would like to go before its over.

6. Their always away during their vacation.

7. Whose tent was standing next to the fire pit?

8. This surfboard is mine because your's has a scratch on the rudder.

9. Its not likely that the game will live up to it's exaggerated promotion.

10. The present was given to me and Lester.

11. They want to know whose going with them.

12. When you take your break, don't forget that it's my turn next.

13. Please save some seats for me and John.

14. Your not going to take that class, are you?

EXERCISE 21B

If a sentence contains an error in pronoun usage, cross out the incorrect pronoun, and write in the correct form. Some sentences may contain more than one error. If a sentence contains no pronoun errors, label it *C* for *correct*. Apply the rules of formal English usage.

1. Anyone who wants a promotion had better do their work carefully.

2. The difference between Connie and myself is that I try hard.

3. Miami is crowded, but it's winter climate is wonderful.

4. If a person goes to New York for the first time, you should not miss the Statue of Liberty.

5. You're never too old to dream.

6. People who haven't paid their dues should expect to lose your privileges.

7. Let's keep this a secret between you and myself.

8. The credit was shared between me and Patricia.

9. When an airline bumps a passenger, they should have to allow the passenger their refund on the spot.

10. Us veterans know better.

11. This handwriting is either Renee's or your's.

12. Does each of the actors know their lines?

13. My uncle, he keeps his secrets to hisself.

14. Just between you and I, this restaurant is a jewel.

Pronoun Usage
Unit Review

Part One   Some of the following sentences contain pronoun errors. Cross out the incorrect pronouns, and write in the correct forms. If a sentence contains no pronoun errors, label it *C* for *correct*. Apply the rules of formal English usage.

1. If someone plans to participate you should give the secretary your name.

2. The college sent my sister and me a catalog.

3. Are you as tired as me?

4. After the World Series next year, we Yankee fans will celebrate.

5. The children remembered more of the movie than him.

6. Either I or my brother will deliver the supplies.

7. Carla wants to know who's boyfriend is missing.

8. Is anybody in the group missing their program?

9. Ms. Rowe asked me and my friend to audition for the talent show.

10. If you're going to visit New Orleans, take along a friend of your's.

11. My friends are going to do their report themselfs.

12. After it's engine has been fixed, Tom's car will sell easily.

Part Two   Correct any pronoun errors that you find in the following paragraph. Apply the rules of formal English usage.

My brother has always been more intellectual than I. Its not that

I don't like to read books or think for myself, but it's a question of priorities. I would rather be hiking, or fishing, or with other people than studying or even reading a book for pleasure. My brother lives in a world of books and ideas. Sometimes I think he would rather argue than eat. His friends and him sometimes argue most of the night. Of course, intellectuals live for ideas, but, between you and me, I believe that many intellectuals, their afraid of life. Some of these big thinkers can't do anything that requires just a little common sense. My brother, he can't even fix a flat tire. Also, I think each person needs a lot of exercise and movement in their life to be healthy and happy. How can someone get any exercise if you stay inside all day and never move anything but you're eyelids?

CAPITALIZATION, MORE PUNCTUATION, PLACEMENT OF MODIFIERS, PARALLEL STRUCTURE, AND IRREGULAR VERBS

22

Capitalization

The general principle behind capitalization is that **proper nouns** (names of *specific* persons, places, or things) are capitalized. **Common nouns** (names of *general* persons, places, or things) are *not* capitalized.

Study the following sentences, each of which illustrates a rule of capitalization.

1. Capitalize all parts of a person's name.

Sandra Day O'Connor is the highest ranking woman judge.

2. Capitalize the titles of relatives only when the titles precede the person's name or when they take the place of a person's name.

*A*unt Louise is a good friend.
Happy birthday, *M*other.
            but
My *u*ncle and my *m*other are both retired.

The same rule applies to professional titles.

I visited *D*r. Wilson at his office.
but
A *d*octor must study for many years before practicing.

3. Capitalize the names of streets, cities, and states.

My uncle lives at 326 *W*right *S*treet, *L*oganville, *O*hio.

4. Capitalize the names of countries, languages, and ethnic groups.

The *L*atvians of *R*ussia speak *R*ussian, but they are trying to get their own language of *L*atvian legalized.

5. Capitalize the names of specific buildings, geographical features, schools, and other institutions.

We visited the *E*mpire *S*tate *B*uilding, *C*entral *P*ark, *C*olumbia *U*niversity, and the *G*uggenheim *M*useum.

6. Capitalize the days of the week, the months of the year, and the names of holidays. Do *not* capitalize the names of the seasons of the year.

We usually celebrate *T*hanksgiving on the last *T*hursday in *N*ovember. I like to see the leaves change color in *a*utumn.

7. Capitalize directions of the compass only when they refer to specific regions.

Just when she became used to the warm winters of the *S*outhwest, her company transferred her *n*orth to Minneapolis.

8. Capitalize the names of companies and brand names but not the names of the products themselves.

Only the *C*oca-*C*ola *C*ompany can legally manufacture the base for the *s*oft *d*rink *C*oca-*C*ola.
She uses nothing but *T*ide *s*oap.

9. Capitalize the first word of every sentence.

10. Capitalize the subject pronoun *I*.

11. Capitalize the first word of a title and all other words in the title except for articles (*a, an, the*) and except for conjunctions and prepositions that have fewer than five letters.

Who wrote *The Truth about Inflation?*
She sang, *''America the Beautiful.''*

12. Capitalize the names of academic subjects only if they are already proper nouns or if they are common nouns followed by a course number.

I am taking *S*panish, a *h*istory class, and *M*ath 101.

13. Capitalize the names of specific historical events, such as wars, revolutions, religious and political movements, and specific eras.

The *V*ietnam *W*ar, in which the United States sided with South Vietnam, ended in 1975.
During the *G*reat *D*epression, which lasted from 1929 to the early 1940s, many banks failed, and millions of Americans lost their jobs.
The *M*iddle *A*ges, a long period of European history, began with the *F*all of *R*ome in the fifth century and lasted for a thousand years until the *R*enaissance.

EXERCISE 22A

Add capital letters to the following sentences wherever they are necessary.

1. didn't you take algebra 101 before you took any chemistry courses from professor brown?

2. send aunt martha's package to her new address at 763 sutter street, boise, idaho; i'm not sure of the zip code.

3. many of the horror novels of stephen king, such as *pet sematary*, have been made into films.

4. the war in vietnam, unlike world war II, was not supported by most americans.

5. my grandfather on my mother's side is called ike, and he won't eat any chili except hormel's chili.

6. i wish that holidays like lincoln's birthday were celebrated on the actual day of birth instead of on the nearest monday or friday.

7. we drive north on highway 101, crossing the golden gate bridge in san francisco and continuing all the way to the oregon border.

8. yes, i do believe dr. gordon is a good doctor, but her specialty at memorial hospital is hematology, not dermatology.

9. our friends from england enjoyed their visit in the south, but it took them awhile to learn to speak the southern dialect.

10. we crossed the hudson river near new york city, stopped for lunch at some county park, and then took some pictures with our new kodak of the place where abraham lincoln gave his famous gettysburg address near the end of the civil war.

11. mary speaks spanish though she's never been to spain, but john knows only a few words of french though he lived many months in paris.

EXERCISE 22B

Add capital letters to the following sentences wherever they are necessary.

The olympic games are the premier athletic contest for most of earth's people. In seoul, south korea, during the summer of 1988, nearly 20,000 athletes from almost two hundred countries competed for seventeen days to determine who were the world's fastest, strongest, most graceful athletes.

The original olympic games took place about 2,765 years ago in ancient greece. The greek games began as footraces, but as time went on, more events like boxing and wrestling were added. No women were allowed to witness or take part in these games; however, by the sixth century b.c., the women had begun their own games, called the *heraea.* the greek games continued for over 1,100 years, but as they become increasingly professionalized, they lost their original appeal to amateurs. A roman, emperor theodosius, discontinued the greek games at the end of the fourth century a.d.

The modern olympics had their start in 1896 under the leadership of baron coubertin of france, who convinced a number of countries to meet in athens, greece, in a contemporary version of the ancient games. Today both the summer and winter games are organized and controlled by the international olympic committee. A smaller committee in each member country regulates the selection and training of its athletes.

It has not been possible to keep politics out of the modern games. Countries keep "score" of the medals, especially the gold ones, that their athletes win. And worse, many countries and groups have treated the olympics as a political arena where they can play to a worldwide audience. In 1980 the united states boycotted the moscow olympics to protest the russian invasion of afghanistan. In 1988, north korea and some of its allies stayed away from the games in south korea. the most tragic political use of the games came at 1972 in munich, germany, when nine members of the israeli team were kidnapped and later murdered by arab terrorists.

Neither the dangers of politicization nor the massive costs of staging the games every four years have lessened the fundamental appeal of the olympics. Today the i.o.c. has many countries waiting to host the games in the twenty-first century.

EXERCISE 22C

Some capitalization rules include exceptions to the rule. For each of the rules listed below, write one sentence of your own that illustrates both the rule *and* its exception.

1. The rule about the names of academic subjects:

_____

_____

2. The rule about directions of the compass:

_____

_____

3. The rule about the titles of relatives:

_____

_____

4. The rule about words in the title of a book, movie, television program, and so on:

_____

_____

5. The rule about companies and brand names:

_____

_____

6. The rule about periods of time, such as days of the week, months of the year:

_____

_____

7. The rule about professional titles:

_____

_____

23

More on Punctuation

We learned in Lesson 11 to put a comma after an introductory dependent clause. At certain other times it is customary to separate **introductory** material from an independent clause which follows it.

> *According to the latest research*, your answer is correct. (introductory prepositional phrase)
> *Sliding across home plate*, he scored the winning run. (introductory participial phrase)

It is also customary to separate coordinate adjectives modifying the same noun. (Adjectives are *coordinate* if you can substitute *and* for the comma.)

> Mary is a happy, thoughtful person.
> or
> Mary is a happy *and* thoughtful person.

We learned in earlier lessons to use commas to set off appositives and parenthetical expressions. However, when the writer wishes to emphasize the importance or abruptness of such words, a **dash** may be used.

Nat loved only one person — himself.

Patty won — would you believe it? — six times in a row.

The **colon** is sometimes confused with the semicolon because of the similarity in names, but the two marks function differently. In addition to the colon's mechanical use to separate hours from minutes (8:45) and chapters from verses (*Genesis* 2:5), this mark is used frequently to introduce lists, summaries, series, and quotations which may be of almost any length or form. (Notice that what follows the **colon** is not necessarily an independent clause, that is, it may be fragmentary.)

Janey's backpack contained everything she would need for the hike: suntan lotion, a first aid kit, a bathing suit and towel, and a snack.

The secret to success in retailing may be summed up in three words: *location, location, location.*

Shakespeare said it so well: "Ripeness is all."

For an example of a colon introducing a summary, see p. 134.

An **apostrophe** with an *s* (*'s* or *s'*) on nouns and indefinite pronouns makes those words possessive. For most singular nouns or indefinite pronouns add the apostrophe followed by *s*.

Jill*'s* hair

the boy*'s* appearance

someone*'s* bicycle

John*'s* and Mary*'s* lunch

But if the singular noun ends in an *s*, *sh*, or a *z* sound, add either the apostrophe alone or an apostrophe and another *s*.

Le*s'* book or Les*'s* book

jazz*'* origins or jazz*'s* origins

For most plural nouns (those ending in an *s*, *sh*, or *z* sound), use the apostrophe alone.

the Joneses*'* car

the cats*'* fights

the ladies*'* dresses

But for a plural noun not ending in an *s*, *sh*, or *z* sound, add *'s*.

the children*'s* laughter

Sometimes possession is indicated by both the apostrophe and *of* in a prepositional phrase.

That book *of* Tom*'s* is over here.

And a possessive may follow the word it modifies.

Is this book Tom*'s*?

Direct quotations make writing vivid. Long direct quotations as in research papers, are indented and single spaced, but most direct quotes are simply enclosed in **quotation marks.**

''Come inside and have some coffee.''

If the quotation is part of a longer sentence, it is set off by commas.

She said, ''Come inside and have some coffee.''
''I know,'' said the old man, ''that you want me to go.''

Three rules govern the use of quotation marks with other forms of punctuation:

1. The comma and period are *always* enclosed within quotation marks.

''I like you,'' she said, ''but I don't love you.''

2. The colon and semicolon are *never* enclosed within quotation marks.

He tried to sing, ''Chloe''; but he didn't know the words.

3. Question marks, exclamation marks, and dashes are *within* the quotation marks if they apply to the quoted material and *after* the quotation marks if they apply to the whole sentence.

"Is he your friend?" Matt asked.
Did Matt say, "It's time to eat"?

You may have noticed in the discussion of capitalization that some titles are shown between quotation marks: "America the Beautiful," and some titles are shown in italics: *The Truth about Inflation.* The choice between these two ways to indicate titles is generally based on the length of the work so titled. The titles of minor works such as songs, short poems and stories, essays and articles in periodicals, and episodes of a series are put between **quotation marks.** The titles of longer works, and complete volumes or complete series are put in **italics.**

Italics are a special slanted typeface used by printers. In the handwritten and typewritten papers of most students, italics must be indicated by *underlining.*

I photocopied Frost's poem, "Birches" from *The Complete Poems of Robert Frost.*
See the chapter "Genetics" in the text *Modern Biology.*
One of her sources was the article, "Women at Work" in the *New York Times.*
They sang the duet "People Will Say We're in Love" from *Oklahoma.*

EXERCISE 23A

Add commas, colons, dashes, quotation marks, apostrophes, and italics to the following sentences wherever they are necessary. (Indicate italics by *underlining*.)

1. According to my latest calculations your answer is correct.

2. Feeling like a flying fish Leah sailed her windsurfer off the crest of the wave.

3. The tall handsome stranger rode a white horse.

4. My neighbor won the jackpot in the lottery three million dollars.

5. A good wrestler needs three qualities balance speed and strength.

6. That girls bike was stolen, but Mannys bike was returned.

7. The three brothers noses were shaped like pigs snouts.

8. I asked him Do you want more cake ?

9. Her daughter wrote a poem called Spring, which was accepted by Poetry magazine.

10. After the setting of the sun a bugler played Taps.

11. All of the Joneses entries were winners in the contest.

12. You didn't follow the rules, said the judge, so I must disqualify you !

13. My favorite proverb is very brief You only live once !

14. Looking quickly through the third volume of The Encyclopedia Britannica Harold found the short article entitled Copper.

15. Louis and Irenes style is very smooth and flowing, but the other couples movements make La Bamba seem like a military march.

16. The band played The Star Spangled Banner; then the teams trotted on the field to begin the big game.

EXERCISE 23B

Add capital letters, commas, dashes, apostrophes, colons, periods, quotation marks, and italics to the following sentences wherever they are necessary. (Indicate italics by *underlining*.)

1. marie learned to speak french in canada, but she will use it this summer in france.

2. john told alice that he never wanted to see her again.

3. john told alice i never want to see you again.

4. the jazz pianist nellie foster played a steinway piano.

5. of all the doctors at the clinic she liked dr. hill best.

6. if you serve uncle joe any cereal but yummies he will shout are you trying to kill me?

7. willy dropped one of his math courses and signed up for introduction to aerobics because he saw the new aerobics teacher ms betty jones.

8. when sammy castros grandfather died sammy kept the congressional medal of honor which his grandfather had won for storming a german machine-gun nest during the d-day invasion of france in world war two.

9. as swanson entered the office door of his companys president for the first time he was shocked to see behind the desk the one person he had never expected to see again his long-lost brother!

10. tina has read all of her christmas present the complete works of william shakespeare except for two plays the tradegy hamlet prince of denmark and the comedy much ado about nothing.

11. i knew my brother tony was planning a surprise birthday party for me when he said hi sis how about coming over to my place for an italian dinner? because i know he hates to cook.

12. the only way to answer this question said our psychology professor dr blume is for us to have the whole group meet over coffee some tuesday night and speak frankly with one another.

13. the browns subscribe to the los angeles times for several reasons pogo doonesbury the crossword puzzle and the daily column by jack smith.

14. the joneses cat and their new neighbors dog have been fighting for territory ever since the neighbors moved in on the fourth of july.

15. i remember reading an article about this topic last summer; it was called guns for sale and im sure i read it in the new yorker magazine.

16. bring these items to the examination a pen your textbook at least a dozen sheets of lined notebook paper and perhaps a dictionary.

17. we will drive west on our vacation, stopping briefly in denver and then angling north to portland and seattle, the largest cities of the northwest.

24

Misplaced and Dangling Modifiers

Modifiers are words that are used to describe other words in a sentence. A modifier may be a single word, a phrase, or a clause. (Adjective clauses are discussed in Lesson 14.) Examples of some of the more common types of modifiers are given below. Circle the word that each italicized modifier describes.

ADJECTIVE   The dancer wore a *red* dress.

ADJECTIVE CLAUSE   The woman *who is speaking* is the chairperson.

PREPOSITIONAL PHRASE   The book *on the table* is my text.

The words you should have circled are *dress*, which is modified by "red," *woman*, which is modified by "who is speaking," and *book*, which is modified by "on the table."

Another type of modifier is a **participial phrase.** A participial phrase begins with a participle. A **participle** is a verb form that functions as an adjective. There are two kinds of participles. **Present participles** are formed by adding

-ing to the main verb (for example, *walking, knowing, seeing.*) **Past participles** are the verb forms that are used with the helping verb *have* (have *walked*, have *known*, have *seen*). Circle the word that each of the following participial phrases modifies.

Knowing the answer, Rebecca raised her hand.

A movie *directed by this man* has won an Oscar.

The words that you should have circled are *Rebecca* and *movie*.

If you look back at all the words that you have circled so far in this lesson, you will notice that although modifiers sometimes precede and sometimes follow the words they describe, they are in all cases placed as close as possible to the word that they describe. Failure to place a modifier in the correct position in a sentence results in an error known as a **misplaced modifier.**

MISPLACED   Ray bought a hamburger for his friend *with lots of onions.* (Does Ray's friend have lots of onions?)

CORRECT   Ray bought a hamburger *with lots of onions* for his friend.

MISPLACED   They gave an award to the athlete *plated with gold.* (Was the athlete plated with gold?)

CORRECT   They gave a trophy *plated with gold* to the athlete.

Correct the misplaced modifiers in the following sentences.

We used a poster for the dance painted in blues and greens.

Jack purchased his boat from a dealer that had a rebuilt engine.

I gave a party for my friend that will never be forgotten.

An error related to the misplaced modifier is the **dangling modifier.** A dangling modifier sometimes occurs when a participial phrase is placed at the beginning of a sentence. A participial phrase in this position *must describe the subject of the following clause.* If the subject of the clause cannot logically perform the action described in the participial phrase, the phrase is said to "dangle" (to hang loosely, without a logical connection).

DANGLING   *After leaving here,* his troubles lessened. (This sentence suggests that his *troubles* left here.)

CORRECT   After *he* left here, his troubles lessened.

DANGLING   *While laughing at me,* Sam's pants fell off. (This sentence suggests that Sam's *pants* were laughing.)

CORRECT   While *Sam* was laughing at me, his pants fell off.

Notice that there are several ways to correct dangling modifiers. You may add a noun or pronoun to the sentence to provide a word that the modifier can logically describe, or you may reword the entire sentence. *However, simply reversing the order of the dangling modifier and the rest of the sentence does not correct the error.*

DANGLING   When smiling, her teeth sparkle.

STILL DANGLING   Her teeth sparkle when smiling.

CORRECT   When she is smiling, her teeth sparkle.

Revise the following sentences so that they no longer contain dangling modifiers.

Driving down the street, Larry's car struck a lamppost.

Waiting for a promotion, his job drove him crazy.

While listening to the radio, my foot fell asleep.

When feeling happy, her future looks bright.

Because misplaced and dangling modifiers create confusing and even absurd sentences, you should be careful to avoid them in your writing.

EXERCISE 24A

Part One Construct five sentences of your own, using the modifiers listed below at the beginning of your sentences. Make certain that your modifiers do not dangle.

1. Not knowing which way to turn, _____

_____

2. After lasting nine rounds, _____

_____

3. By going the scenic route, _____

_____

4. In order to guarantee the result, _____

_____

5. When smelling that perfume, _____

_____

6. Losing your head and falling head over heels in love, _____

_____

Part Two Rewrite each of the following sentences so that none contains a dangling or misplaced modifier.

7. Manny gave a gift to his girl that he wrapped himself. _____

_____

8. They go to the races on all the sunny days that are held in Belmont Park. _____

_____

9. When cashing the check, his pen stopped working. _____

_____

10. Knowing the words to the song, our voices rang out clearly.

_____

_____

11. We gave a present to our boss that we wrapped in the prettiest pink bows.

_____

_____

12. After cooking the dinner, the dishes needed to be done. _____

_____

13. Once glued, you must allow the finished pieces to sit for at least six

hours. _____

_____

14. Eager to finish the job, a sudden rain changed all our plans.

_____

_____

15. When told the truth, Sally's expression was shocked. _____

_____

16. Reacting like a rebellious teenager, my father made me toe the line.

_____

_____

EXERCISE 24B

Some of the following sentences contain misplaced modifiers or dangling modifiers. Rewrite these sentences. If a sentence is correctly constructed, label it *C* for *correct*.

1. When replacing this part, your tools must be grounded.

_____

_____

2. Not having made any payments for three months, she must satisfy her creditors or lose her car.

_____

_____

3. He left thousands of dollars to the children that he had counterfeited.

_____

_____

4. Smiling one of his famous smiles, the recording star signed his autograph.

_____

_____

5. To be admitted to that college, good grades and high scores on the entrance tests are a necessity.

_____

_____

6. Martha located the recipe looking at the cookbook.

_____

_____

7. Instead of eating lemon chiffon pie, a German chocolate cake was served.

_____

_____

8. While watching the basketball game, the crowd cheered with an enthusiasm that knew no bounds.

_____

_____

9. To open a checking account, your first deposit must be at least two hundred dollars.

_____

_____

10. He asked for an item that was cooked to order with an air of nonchalance.

_____

_____

11. Feeling the pain of divorce, he drowned his sorrows in gin.

_____

_____

12. She memorialized the day that she had met William with a page in her scrapbook.

_____

_____

25

Parallel Structure

The term **parallel structure** means that similar ideas should be expressed in similar grammatical structures. For example, Benjamin Franklin quoted the following proverb:

Early to bed and early to rise make a man healthy, wealthy, and wise.

This proverb is a good illustration of parallel structure. It begins with two similar phrases, "early to bed" and "early to rise," and it ends with a series of three similar words (they are all adjectives): *healthy, wealthy,* and *wise.*

In contrast, the following two versions of the same proverb contain some words that are *not* parallel.

Early to bed and early *rising* make a man healthy, wealthy, and wise.
Early to bed and early to rise make a man healthy, wealthy, and *give wisdom.*

Therefore, these last two sentences are *not* properly constructed.

Since there are many different grammatical structures in the English language, the possibilities for constructing non-parallel sentences may appear to be almost unlimited. Fortunately, you do not have to be able to identify all the grammatical structures in a sentence in order to tell whether or not that sentence has parallel structure. Sentences that lack parallel structure are usually so awkward that they are easy to recognize.

NOT PARALLEL I enjoy *swiming, surfing,* and *to sail.*
PARALLEL I enjoy *swimming, surfing,* and *sailing.*
NOT PARALLEL The doctor told me *to stay* in bed, *that I should drink* lots of liquids, and *to take* two aspirins every four hours.
PARALLEL The doctor told me *to stay* in bed, *to drink* lots of liquids, and *to take* two aspirins every four hours.
NOT PARALLEL He wrote *quickly, carefully,* and *with clarity.*
PARALLEL He wrote *quickly, carefully,* and *clearly.*

Revise each of the following sentences so that it is parallel in structure.

Potatoes can be boiled, baked, or you can fry them.

The movie was a success because of its good acting, interesting plot, and

its special effects were exciting.

Please list your name, how old you are, and your birthplace.

The Admissions Office told me to read the college catalog and that I should

make an appointment with a counselor.

Some errors in parallel structure occur when a writer is not careful in the use of correlative conjunctions. **Correlative conjunctions** are conjunctions that occur in pairs, such as:

both . . . and
either . . . or
neither . . . nor
not only . . . but also

Since these conjunctions occur in pairs, they are usually used to compare two ideas. For example:

Her workout was *neither* tedious *nor* tiring.

Correctly used, correlative conjunctions will structure a sentence in effective parallel form.

The rule for using correlative conjunctions is that the conjunctions *must be placed as close as possible to the words that are being compared.* For example:

I will choose *either* the yellow shirt *or* the green one.

not

I *either* will choose the yellow shirt *or* the green one.

Study the following examples of correctly and incorrectly placed correlative conjunctions.

INCORRECT   You *not only* need to see a doctor *but also* a lawyer.
  CORRECT   You need to see *not only* a doctor *but also* a lawyer.
INCORRECT   She *both* speaks French *and* Italian.
  CORRECT   She speaks *both* French *and* Italian.

Correct the misplaced correlative conjunctions in the following sentences.

He will go neither with his mother or stay with his sister.

These old chairs both are comfortable and durable.

They not only traveled to the moon but also on to Jupiter.

You either ought to see less of her or marry her.

EXERCISE 25A

Rewrite any sentences that lack parallel structure. If a sentence is already parallel, label it *C* for *correct*.

1. Wash the car, wax it, and vacuum the interior.

   _____

   _____

2. Her performance was well conceived, well rehearsed, and had good execution. _____

   _____

3. They neither avoided the traffic jam nor the detour.

   _____

   _____

4. In order to guarantee the result, we also counted the cash by hand and double-checked our addition.

   _____

   _____

5. When smelling that perfume, close your eyes, inhale its fragrance, and that you are imagining your beloved.

   _____

   _____

6. The green-eyed, brunette contestant, who was tall, did very well in the talent division.

   _____

   _____

7. Manny not only gave a gift but also a card to his girlfriend.

_____

_____

8. They go to the races neither expecting to win money nor for the excitement, but they just wish to be outdoors on a nice summer day.

_____

_____

9. To visit Tahiti is to see paradise.

_____

_____

10. Brian was not what she had expected in a husband but the kind of man she could grow to love.

_____

_____

11. The spectators began to feel restless and that they were being victimized.

_____

_____

12. She wanted three things: to be needed, to be loved, and a way to feel accepted as an adult.

_____

_____

13. Either they follow instructions or they lose their jobs.

_____

_____

EXERCISE 25B

Rewrite any sentences that lack parallel structure or that contain misplaced or dangling modifiers. If a sentence needs no revision, label it *C* for *correct*.

1. When using this paint, the surface must be absolutely clean and dry.

_____

_____

2. She either must improve her results or lose the competition.

_____

_____

3. He sent copies of the negatives to his relatives that he had developed.

_____

_____

4. Baking one of her delicious pies, grandma proved she was as good a cook as she had ever been.

_____

_____

5. To be admitted to that college, Johnny not only made good grades but also scored well on the entrance tests.

_____

_____

6. Knowing all the right answers, the test was easy.

_____

_____

7. Whether in control or when he was only horsing around, Jessie was the best player on the court.

_____

_____

8. She was happy and in an optimistic state of mind after the interview.

_____

_____

9. His life was influenced by not only his genetic makeup but also by what had happened in his environment.

_____

_____

10. Ignored by her host and the other guests, Elaine did not enjoy the party.

_____

_____

11. The greatest threat to the organization was not the lazy, ignorant members but the industrious members who were ignorant.

_____

_____

12. Mac had no money for luxuries or to by warm clothes.

_____

_____

26

Irregular Verbs

Verbs have three **principal** (meaning "most important") **parts:** the *present* (which, when preceded by *to,* becomes the *infinitive*), the *past,* and the *past participle.*

The **present** form may stand alone as a main verb without any helping verb. For example:

I *live* in California.
Many students *ride* the bus to school.

It may also be preceded by a helping verb, such as *can, could, do, does, did, may, might, must, shall, should, will,* or *would.* (A list of helping verbs appears in Lesson 4, p. 38.)

John *should see* a doctor.
She *may need* a new car.

However, the present form is *not* used after any forms of the helping verbs *have (has, have, had)* or *be (am, is, are, was, were, been).*

The **past** form is used alone as a main verb. It is *not* preceded by a helping verb when expressing the simple past tense.

Our friends *left* town yesterday.
The class *began* twenty minutes ago.

The **past participle** is *always* preceded by at least one, and sometimes more than one, helping verb. The helping verb is often a form of *have* or *be*.

I *have washed* the car.
The vegetables *were grown* in our garden.

Most English verbs are regular. A **regular** verb forms both its past and past participle by adding -*ed* to the present. (If the present already ends in -*e*, only a -*d* is added.)

Present	*Past*	*Past Participle*
talk	talked	talked
like	liked	liked

Any verb that does *not* form both its past and past participle by adding -*ed* or -*d* is considered **irregular.** For example:

Present	*Past*	*Past Participle*
eat	ate	eaten
write	wrote	written
begin	began	begun

Study the sentences below. Notice that the differences between regular and irregular verbs are not apparent in the present tense and that, with regular verbs, the *past* and the *past participle* are spelled alike.

REGULAR   IRREGULAR

present tense

I *live* here.   I *eat* pizza.
I *walk* my dog.   I *am* a student.
We *rent* this place.   I *write* essays.
                                        We *begin* the project today.

(continued)

past tense

I *lived* here.

I *walked* my dog.

We *rented* this place.

I *ate* pizza.

I *was* a student.

I *wrote* essays.

We *began* the project yesterday.

present perfect tense (with past participle)

I *have lived* here.

I *have walked* my dog.

We *have rented* this place.

I *have eaten* pizza.

I *have been* a student.

I *have written* essays.

We *have begun* the project.

past perfect tense (with past participle)

I *had lived* here.

I *had walked* my dog.

We *had rented* this place.

I *had eaten* pizza before then.

I *had been* a student in 1987.

I *had written* essays before I knew her.

We *had begun* the project before the storm hit.

Since irregular verbs by definition have irregular spellings, you must *memorize* the spelling of their past and past participle forms. Irregular verbs include many of the most commonly used verbs in the English language (for example, *come, go, eat, drink, sit, stand*), so it is important to study them carefully.

Here is a list of some of the most commonly used irregular verbs. In addition to learning the verbs on this list, if you are not sure whether or not a verb is irregular, look it up in the dictionary. A good dictionary will list the principal parts of an irregular verb in addition to defining its meaning.

Present	Past	Past Participle			
beat	beat	beaten	bring	brought	brought
begin	began	begun	build	built	built
bend	bent	bent	buy	bought	bought
bleed	bled	bled	catch	caught	caught
blow	blew	blown	choose	chose	chosen
break	broke	broken	come	came	come

cut	cut	cut	read	read	read
do	did	done	ride	rode	ridden
draw	drew	drawn	ring	rang	rung
drink	drank	drunk	rise	rose	risen
drive	drove	driven	run	ran	run
eat	ate	eaten	see	saw	seen
fall	fell	fallen	sell	sold	sold
feed	fed	fed	send	sent	sent
feel	felt	felt	set	set	set
find	found	found	shake	shook	shaken
fly	flew	flown	shoot	shot	shot
freeze	froze	frozen	sing	sang	sung
get	got	got *or* gotten	sink	sank	sunk
give	gave	given	sit	sat	sat
go	went	gone	sleep	slept	slept
grow	grew	grown	speak	spoke	spoken
have	had	had	spend	spent	spent
hear	heard	heard	spin	spun	spun
hide	hid	hidden	stand	stood	stood
hit	hit	hit	steal	stole	stolen
hurt	hurt	hurt	stick	stuck	stuck
keep	kept	kept	swear	swore	sworn
know	knew	known	swim	swam	swum
lay	laid	laid	take	took	taken
leave	left	left	teach	taught	taught
lend	lent	lent	tear	tore	torn
lie	lay	lain	tell	told	told
lose	lost	lost	think	thought	thought
make	made	made	throw	threw	thrown
mean	meant	meant	wear	wore	worn
meet	met	met	weep	wept	wept
pay	paid	paid	win	won	won
put	put	put	write	wrote	written

Notice that compound verbs follow the same pattern as their root form. For example:

be*come*	be*came*	be*come*
for*give*	for*gave*	for*given*
under*stand*	under*stood*	under*stood*

EXERCISE 26A

Circle the verb form that correctly completes each sentence. If you are not absolutely certain of the correct form, go back to the list of irregular verbs *before* you make your choice.

1. Have they (did, done) all the homework?

2. She has (drove, driven) 845 miles since yesterday.

3. Tom has (swam, swum) across the pool.

4. His folks (was, were) happy about the marriage.

5. A hen that has (laid, layed) an egg will cackle.

6. Lily has (drank, drunk) the whole pitcher.

7. We have (choosed, chosen) our next president.

8. Has Mabel ever (sung, sang) without accompaniment?

9. We have (ate, eaten) the dinner.

10. Had Teresa ever (ran, run) the mile before?

11. She (become, became) a grandmother.

12. They have (builded, built) too close to the river.

13. We had (flew, flown) with that airline many times.

14. Had he really (brung, brought) a dog into church?

15. The fastest horse has (winned, won) the race.

16. Larry has (teached, taught) many children to swim.

17. We have (give, given) it our best.

18. Stan (known, knew) the right thing to do.

19. Roger has (laid, lied, lain, layed) there since noon.

20. She has (sworn, swore) to tell the truth.

21. The flower pot had (sat, set) there for a week.

22. That child had (grew, grown, growed) like a weed.

23. They have (rode, ridden) their bikes across the new lawn.

24. Have they (broke, broken) the record yet?

Capitalization, More Punctuation, Placement of Modifiers, Parallel Structure, and Irregular Verbs Unit Review

Part One   Add any missing capitals, commas, quotation marks, apostrophes, or italics to the following paragraphs. Correct any misplaced or dangling modifiers, and restructure any faulty parallelism.

1.   rene descartes, a frenchman, was a philosopher who wrote during the historical period known as the enlightenment. He believed that unaided reason ought to be able to explain and would demonstrate the workings of the universe. descartes is famous for the saying i think; therefore, i am.

2.   who said from each according to his ability; to each according to his need. wasnt it karl marx? isnt it from marxs book das kapital that attacks capitalism and is an argument in favor of communism?

3.   pablo neruda typifies the literary figure of latin america. neruda a highly educated chilean spoke a variety of languages besides his native spanish. he served his government in many different capacities. he served in europe for example as an ambassador. he never withheld his strong political opinions and was outspoken in expressing them. he not only was a noted essayist but also a great poet. he will probably be best

remembered for collections of poems like cantos de amor and as one of the greatest latin american poets.

4. do as i say; not as i do. that proverb might be called hypocritical or expressing a cynical point of view. but doesn't that interpretation depend on the tone of voice or of the context in which the proverb is used? after all one could argue that the speakers intention really expresses an attempt to be honest or to have self-awareness.

5. attila the hun ruled the huns in the fifth century a.d. under his powerful personality and with his leadership the huns overran huge areas of eastern and central europe. the cruelty of his armies was legendary to his victims. he liked to be known by the title scourge of god.

Part Two   Correct any improper verb forms in the following paragraphs.

A long time ago, a widowed king had a daughter, an only child, and every man who looked at her thought she was the loveliest woman that he had ever saw. When the time come for the king to find his daughter a husband, the king asked his beautiful daughter if she had meet a man worthy to be her husband. "I have not, father, but let some princely suitor open this casket, and him will I marry."

And she layed at her father's feet a gold casket of surpassing beauty, which no one had ever saw before.

From all the world came brave princes to look upon this maiden princess and win her hand and her throne. Although many tried, no man was able to open the casket and no man could take the princess for his bride. After several years, from a far country traveled three brothers, princes from a small kingdom. They brung no gifts for the princess, for their kingdom had growed poor from many wars. The oldest of the three must have been the strongest man alive, for when he met the princess, he raise her on her throne high in the air, sat the throne down, and said, "You shall be mine!" But not all his strength could force open the casket, and he left in disgust. The middle prince knowed all the secrets of metals and locks, and he smiled at the princess and said, "My knowledge of secret things will make you mine!" The casket, however, would not open for him, and he stalked angrily away.

When the youngest brother come into the throne room, he walked straight to the princess, bowed low, looked into her eyes and speaked these words, "My lovely princess, all my life I have sought you. If you wish it, the casket shall open for me." And the princess reached into her bodice, near to her heart, drawed out a small, warm, gold key, and give it to him. Then and there they sweared their love to one another. The king drunk a toast to the man his daughter had chose, and all the people sung in happiness.

After the wise prince and his bride were wed, she bore twins, a boy and a girl. And from the stories that were wrote about the children, we know that they were given the names Yang and Yin.

ANSWERS TO "A" EXERCISES

Exercise 1A

1. English is
2. It resembles
3. root is
4. tribes crossed
5. tribes were
6. They conquered
7. land became
8. language evolved
9. invaders came
10. invasion changed
11. invaders added
12. (You) Take
13. conquerors brought
14. English includes

15. <u>English</u> <u>seems</u>
16. <u>languages</u> <u>lent</u>
17. <u>Arabic</u> <u>gave</u>
18. <u>We</u> <u>borrowed</u>
19. <u>vocabulary</u> <u>is</u>
20. <u>Chinese</u> <u>is</u>
21. <u>people</u> <u>speak</u>
22. <u>language</u> <u>opens</u>
23. <u>(You)</u> <u>Learn</u>

Exercise 2A

1. <u>body</u> <u>needs</u>
2. <u>"exercises"</u> <u>do</u>
3. <u>Weightlifting</u> <u>makes</u> / <u>muscles</u> <u>are</u>
4. <u>person</u> <u>has</u> / <u>exercise</u> <u>begins</u>
5. <u>lungs</u> <u>heart</u> <u>take</u> <u>distribute</u>
6. <u>cell</u> <u>needs</u>
7. <u>exercise</u> <u>works</u>
8. <u>work</u> <u>increases</u>
9. <u>efficiency</u> <u>increases</u> / <u>oxygen</u> <u>becomes</u>
10. <u>exercise</u> <u>is</u>
11. <u>Walking</u> <u>running</u> <u>dancing</u> <u>swimming</u> <u>cycling</u> <u>are</u> / <u>they</u> <u>work</u>
12. <u>exercise</u> <u>expends</u>
13. <u>charts</u> <u>show</u>
14. <u>you</u> <u>are</u> / <u>you</u> <u>walk</u>
15. <u>you</u> <u>are</u> / <u>you</u> <u>swim</u>
16. <u>programs</u> <u>appeal</u> / <u>programs</u> <u>bring</u>

Exercise 3A

1. <u>women</u> <u>have</u>
2. <u>leader</u> <u>was</u>
3. <u>Susan</u> <u>Anthony</u> <u>began</u>
4. <u>Anthony</u> <u>became</u> / <u>she</u> <u>began</u>
5. <u>Anthony</u> <u>Elizabeth</u> <u>Stanton</u> <u>were</u>

6. government gave
7. Anthony believed
8. right became
9. she organized wrote campaigned
10. Anthony group went
11. authorities arrested tried found fined
12. She refused fought lost
13. men were
14. Anthony battled
15. Nineteenth Amendment became
16. It granted
17. needs concerns are

Exercise 4A

1. Knowledge helps
2. causes are found / diseases can be traced
3. number have been found
4. studies have revealed
5. infections are found result
6. They occur / bacteria migrate
7. study has discovered
8. Researchers have studied
9. island is (adj. isolated mod. by very) / some have
10. children have / children are discovered
11. percent percent have
12. All were had experienced
13. results are supported
14. researchers are directing (now = adverb)

Exercise 5A

1. medicine is / people have ridiculed
2. Taking has been considered
3. remedy is getting
4. Drinking has been helping

5. scientists have extracted have named
6. processes lead / colchicine seems
7. researchers hope
8. disease attacks leads
9. studies have been conducted
10. researchers are hoping / colchicine attack
11. cells are / sclerosis begins
12. studies look / expanding is proving
13. people have
14. None are / all have
15. remedies have been shown / saffron will prove

Exercise 6A

1. was
2. were
3. was
4. were
5. was
6. no choice necessary
7. was
8. were
9. was
10. were
11. was
12. were
13. no choice necessary
14. were
15. were
16. no choice necessary
17. have
18. were
19. is
20. have

Exercise 7A

1. gets
2. needs
3. was
4. do
5. are
6. are
7. are
8. stand
9. is
10. was
11. Does
12. meet
13. has
14. are
15. is
16. were
17. is
18. is
19. do
20. stands

Exercise 8A

1. were
2. meets
3. Does
4. consists
5. is
6. adds
7. are
8. was
9. has
10. lasts
11. was
12. are
13. was

14. argue
15. is
16. are
17. is
18. Has
19. last

Exercise 9A

1. interfere
2. have
3. were
4. listens
5. has
6. has
7. gets
8. was
9. Does
10. wins
11. were
12. looks
13. are
14. exist
15. look
16. has
17. Do
18. have

Exercise 10A

Answers will vary.

Exercise 11A

1–11. Answers will vary.
12–16. Sample answers (other answers may be correct):
12. We left early because it was raining.
13. Although Lola is my sister, we rarely see each other.
14. The world will have peace when peace is each person's deepest wish.

15. Even though everyone uses grammar all the time, we don't think about it.
16. When we campaigned vigorously for our candidate, we guaranteed her victory.

Exercise 12A

1. , but (because) we were late.
2. , and (although) we had lost.
3. (Although) the car is expensive, ; its
4. , but (after) the candidates debated on national television, it
5. (Although) the shooting took place in broad daylight, it, and
6. (after) its sales dropped, yet
7. (If) her invention succeeds in getting a patent, herself; we
8. exhausted; however, (until) the race was over,
9. apologized, for (as soon as) he did it.
10. (as) it fell; no one survived.
11. discouraged; nevertheless, (since) the project had been her idea,

12–15. Answers will vary.

Exercise 13A

1. 1960s, the "civil   person, the boycott   effective because demonstrations widely seen
2. thousands, civil rights   capital, Martin   world, the political employment, the Civil
3. responses, civil   movement, the Fair
4. accomplished, the civil rights   attention in the
5. credentials, Allan   Court, contending   admissions, thus
6. do, accomplishing   movements, such as . . . movement, using (OR movements such as . . . movement using.)

Exercise 14A

1. it, isn't
2. all, we've

3. speak, in fact,
4. spell, can't we
5. are, however,
6. saying, doesn't
7. true, I know,   hand, a
8. Furthermore, writing
9. centuries; consequently
10. However, because   speakers, it   or, indeed,
11. English, like   Dundee, sometimes
12. English, however,
13. Yes, reader, speaking   writing, but   is, nonetheless,

Exercise 15A

1. plantain, a   banana, is
2. daughter, captain   teams, won
3. bush, *heteromeles acutifolia,*
4. correct
5. Algebra, the   schedule, has
6. correct
7. correct
8. Midway, an   Ocean, was
9. sister, Rosa, is
10. Gabon, as
11. player, Williams,   team, Schwarznegger
12. symphony, the   Symphony, is

Exercise 16A

¶1 correct
¶2 grades, *C*'s and a few *B*'s, and   home, such
¶3 correct
¶4 date, my   Sally, I
¶5 Daddy, Jack   fifteen, but   sixteen, and
¶6 me, I
¶7 friend, but   grades, which   high, dropped   father, who
¶8 year, I   school, and   standards, which   girls, was   wrong, yet
    forgotten, I   lesson, and, perhaps,   husband, and

Exercise 17A (Optional commas are circled.)

1. Wilmington, North Carolina,
2. C
3. old, very beautiful⊙ and
4. , New Mexico,   City, Kansas,   Newark,
5. C
6. plane, watched   heavens⊙ and
7. Sobel,   Lassiter⊙ and
8. problem, the   problem⊙ and
9. C
10. Avenue,   14D,   Yakima,
11. 27, 1928,
12. collecting, butterfly collecting, baseball card collecting⊙ and
13. Terry, his   Marjorie, his   Nathan⊙ and
14. C

Exercise 18A

1. He   her
2. They   him
3. He   them
4. We   you
5. She   me
6. He   us
7. She   them
8. It   us
9. they
10. he
11. she
12. me
13. she
14. We
15. they
16. him
17. her
18. us
19. she
20. they

Exercise 19A

1. they
2. I
3. he
4. me
5. we
6. her
7. he (has)   OR   (they have known) him.
8. I
9. they
10. they
11. I
12. she
13. I
14. picture shows
15. he
16. me
17. her
18. us
19. herself
20. I

Exercise 20A

1. she
2. his
3. she
4. themselves
5. they
6. they
7. he
8. her
9. he
10. She
11. me
12. its
13. they   they   they

Exercise 21A

1. C
2. whose
3. himself
4. Jenny and me
5. it's   it's
6. They're always
7. C
8. yours
9. It's   its
10. Lester and me
11. who's
12. C
13. John and me
14. You're not

Exercise 22A

1. Didn't   Algebra   Professor Brown
2. Send   Aunt Martha's   Sutter Street, Boise, Idaho; I'm
3. Many   Stephen King   *Pet Sematary*
4. The   Vietnam   World War II   Americans
5. My   Ike   Hormel's
6. I   Lincoln's Birthday   Monday or Friday
7. We   Highway   Golden Gate Bridge in San Francisco   Oregon
8. Yes, I   Dr. Gordon   Memorial Hospital
9. Our   England   South   Southern
10. We   Hudson River   New York City   Kodak   Abraham Lincoln
    Gettysburg Address   Civil War
11. Mary   Spanish   Spain   John   French   Paris

Exercise 23A (Optional commas are circled.)

1. calculations,
2. fish,
3. tall,
4. lottery,
5. qualities: balance, speed ⊙ and
6. girl's   Manny's

285

7. brothers'   pigs'
8. him, "Do   cake
9. "Spring"   *Poetry*
10. sun,   "Taps"
11. Joneses'
12. "You   rules,"   judge, "so   you!"
13. brief: "You only live once!"
14. *Encyclopedia Britannica*, Harold   "Copper."
15. Louis' (or Louis's)   Irene's   couple's   "La Bamba"
16. "The Star Spangled Banner";

Exercise 24A

1–6. Answers will vary.
7–16. Sample answers (other answers may be correct):
  7. Manny gave (to) his girl a gift that he wrapped himself.
  8. On all the sunny days, they go to the races that are held in Belmont Park.
  9. When he was cashing the check, his pen stopped working.
  10. Because we knew the words to the song, our voices rang out clearly.
  11. To our boss we gave a present that we wrapped in the prettiest pink bows.
  12. After cooking the dinner, we need to do the dishes.
  13. Once the finished pieces are glued, you must allow them to sit for at least six hours.
  14. Eager to finish our job, we had to change all our plans because of a sudden rainstorm.
  15. When Sally was told the truth, her expression was one of shock.
  16. After I reacted like a rebellious teenager, my father made me toe the line.

Exercise 25A

  1. C
  2. and well executed.
  3. avoided neither
  4. C
  5. and imagine your beloved.
  6. C OR The tall, green-eyed,

7. gave not only a gift but also a card
8. neither for the expectation of winning money nor for the
9. C
10. but was the kind of man
11. restless and victimized.
12. and to be accepted as an adult.
13. C

Exercise 26A

1. done
2. driven
3. swum
4. were
5. laid
6. drunk
7. chosen
8. sung
9. eaten
10. run
11. became
12. built
13. flown
14. brought
15. won
16. taught
17. given
18. knew
19. lain
20. sworn
21. sat
22. grown
23. ridden
24. broken

Index